System3
Thinking

HOW TO CHOOSE WISELY WHEN FACING
DOUBT, DILEMMA, OR DISRUPTION

PETER J WEBB

'*System 3 Thinking* will set you on your way to making wise decisions when uncertainty is high and the consequences are serious, and this could not be more needed than right now.'

Rasmus Hougaard
Founder & CEO of Potential Project
and author of The Mind of the Leader

'It is with pleasure that I highly recommend Peter Webb's book. Peter brings his many years of wisdom and expertise as a psychologist, leadership coach, author, actor, researcher and educator to this exciting new book. This experience has led him to develop the System 3 model – a new kind of decision-making. He explains the System 3 model that will help guide us not only in making decisions but making the best decisions to deliver the best outcomes for our lives. This book would be most valuable to all of us for personal or work-related decision-making. System 3 is a skillset we can all learn to help us become much more confident, wiser decision-makers.'

Professor Avni Sali AM
Founding Director, National Institute of Integrative Medicine
President of the International Council of Integrative Medicine
Member of the Scientific Board of European Congress for
Integrative Medicine

'If ever there was a time the world desperately needed more wisdom, it's now. *System 3 Thinking* reminds us that wisdom is abundant and attainable by all. It provides a clear framework for tackling life's most difficult decisions and a blueprint for a better way forward for humanity. There's a reason that wise people seem calm and content. They are hopeful, and after reading *System 3 Thinking*, so am I.'

Aaron McEwan
VP, Research & Advisory
Gartner

'Peter Webb's book on System 3 Thinking is perfectly timed. In an era of unprecedented, uncertain change, relying on analytics or gut instinct and past experience for decision-making no longer works. System 3 Thinking is the key to moving forward successfully in this new world. Blending engaging personal stories, academic research and practical action-oriented frameworks, Peter's book is not only an essential guide to wise decision-making, but provides a philosophy for living in the 21st century.'

Jonathan Knight
CEO, Ososim

'If you are like most people, you've probably made a critical decision. You rationally considered all the facts and options, thinking that you were spot-on in your choice, only to have it blow-up in your face. What went wrong? In his book, *System 3 Thinking*, Peter Webb skillfully unpacks what went wrong. Starting with his explanation of how every decision we make is affected by bias, Peter introduces the concept of System 3 Thinking and outlines how, when the consequences of a decision are serious, we can make a Wise Decision.'

Michael E. Kossler
Director Leadership Development
OneAmerica

'There is so much I love about this book. Your ability to draw on your personal experiences in an entertaining way. The honesty in telling your own story and applying it to the approach. The practicality of using robust academic insight and applying it to pragmatic frameworks that can be easily used. I've read *Thinking Fast and Slow* and *Nudge* and always felt there was something missing in the way they articulate behavioural economics. It feels like you have helped uncover the missing link!'

Dominic Walsh
Managing Partner
HERO

'Finally, a book that puts forward a meticulously structured framework for System 3 Thinking! In essence, Peter tells us that decision-making is not symmetrical and neat, but asymmetrical and dynamic. Notwithstanding, by applying the dimensions of System 3 Thinking through the lens of the WISE framework, one can develop a daily practice of wisdom. Thanks to the fruits of his labour, we now have a pragmatic approach that we can adopt for making optimal choices and resolving thorny issues. Foremost, Peter has dug deep into the trenches of his personal experiences and generated insights that snugly dovetail with the philosophy of the primal human activity of decision-making. In sum, this book is a must-read for anyone endeavouring to catalyse constructive decisions when sifting through the options. Read it once or maybe twice (as I surely will) for a reinforcement of the main ideas.'

Geraldine Anita Joseph
Senior Analyst for Leadership and Governance,
The South East Asian Central Banks (SEACEN) Research
and Training Centre

'I enjoyed Peter's book on two levels: personally and professionally. The former because stories told in his book brought back memories of our time together at the ICLIF Leadership and Governance Centre. They remind me how excited Peter would get when uncovering and piecing together the jigsaw of this work. On the professional front, I believe Peter is onto something. Renowned neuroscientist Tara Swart of MIT Sloan School of Management has aptly described the brain as four networks: Control, Affect, Reward, and Default. While the first three are relatively well understood, the last one is perhaps the most intriguing. At the moment, we only know the default network as a myriad of neuro-connections responsible for our introspection and creativity. But we have not quite learned how it does that, or more importantly, how we can optimize its task. Peter's proposed System 3 Thinking is a great step forward in the direction of leveraging what arguably makes the human mind unique and beautiful.'

Dr Thun Thamrongnawasawat
Professor of Practice, Asia School of Business
International Faculty Fellow, MIT Sloan

Acknowledgements

The wise person thinks himself a fool, but the fool thinks he knows everything. So, I confess to feeling rather foolish in attempting to explain how to think wisely. My excuse is that many researchers far cleverer than me have paved the way to explaining the science and psychology of wisdom and how to apply it. I am grateful to the work of the Max Planck Institute for Human Development Berlin, the University of Chicago Center for Practical Wisdom, the University of Waterloo Ontario Wisdom and Culture Lab, the Evidence-based Wisdom site, and the University of California San Diego Center for Healthy Aging.

I am deeply grateful to Professor Tony Grant who set up the Coaching Psychology Unit at the University of Sydney, and who encouraged me to take psychology seriously again, even though 'it's not rocket science'. Your eccentric genius is sorely missed, Tony. Thanks to my colleague Dr Paula Robinson at the Positive Psychology Institute for introducing me to Dr Barry Partridge at the University of Wollongong. Our five-year working partnership laid out the evidence for a third system of thinking. Thank you to my colleagues and friends at ICLIF (International Centre for Leadership in Finance), now the ICLIF Executive Education Centre at the Asia School of Business in Kuala Lumpur, Malaysia. You showed me the true meaning of *Kerjasama* (collaboration). Thanks to Ethan Sagan-Chang, my research assistant for helping to validate the T3 Profile. Thank you to Jonathan Knight and Elisa Alabaster at Ososim for the development of the Complex-city simulation for making wise decisions in the age of disruption. Who knew just how disrupted things would get! Grateful thanks to Juliet Bourke and Connie Hansen for welcoming me back to Deloitte after my sojourn in Asia. You offered me a bridge, although the pandemic would later sweep it away. And thanks to Amanada Quealy, CEO at the National Institute of Integrative Medicine for offering me a home to practise integrative psychology when I was 'homeless'.

I've had this book rattling around in my head for years. Thank you to all my clients, patients, and colleagues for insisting I write it. And huge, enormous thanks to book mentor Kath Walters for squeezing it out of me (in a nice way) in such a short time. Although I lost my way a bit through the pandemic and successive lockdowns, I think I found a wider group of readers to appeal to. I hope so. We all need the skills of choosing wisely when we've run out of options and there's no one to turn to. Thank you to Michael Kossler and Shannon Sweeney for your critical and insightful feedback. Made all the difference to readability. Sincere thanks to Michael Hanrahan and Anna Clemann at Publish Central for deftly steering the manuscript from draft to print. You made the process seamless.

I'm thankful to my father for teaching me to read before I attended school. You were right. It's been a huge advantage throughout my life. I'm thankful to my mother for introducing me to the storytelling of theatre. And I'm profoundly thankful for the gift of my wife, Betty Rose, for her enduring love and fierce loyalty. You have helped me shape a personal practice of wisdom. In the end, I dedicate this book to my children's children's children. May you choose wisely.

Disclaimer

The material in this publication is of the nature of general comment only, and does not represent professional advice. It is not intended to provide specific guidance for particular circumstances and it should not be relied on as the basis for any decision to take action or not take action on any matter which it covers. Readers should obtain professional advice where appropriate, before making any such decision. To the maximum extent permitted by law, the author and publisher disclaim all responsibility and liability to any person, arising directly or indirectly from any person taking or not taking action based on the information in this publication.

Contents

Foreword   xi

Introduction: Moments of choice   1

1. How your choices get hijacked   9

2. System 3 thinking explained   23

3. How to enhance your system 3 thinking   49

4. When choices go bad   85

5. The WISE Framework for making better decisions   111

6. Creating a brighter future   131

Conclusion: Your moment of choice   151

Bibliography   156

Foreword

As I sit in my home office among the gum trees of the Dandenong rainforest east of Melbourne, there are construction workers stopping cars and blocking the Westgate Bridge on the other side of town. They are protesting a decision by the state government to temporarily close down construction due to the increase of COVID-19 cases at building sites and a significant number of workers' refusal to get vaccinated. Speaking to an old friend of mine, I shared with him how easy it is for me to label these people as young men acting out their narcissistic tendencies, to be thinking only of themselves and reverting to violence. I asked him, 'What are the responsibilities of those of us who have been on the path of personal growth and introspection to society?' Based on evidence-based research and from years of experience as a professional practitioner in various fields, Peter's book provides very valuable tools and insights to help me answer this question.

What you will find in the following pages are the keen insights of an intelligent researcher's attempt to make the practice of wisdom more explicit and available to all of us. We need to be able to discern the truth and make better decisions. There is no need to remind you of the volatile, uncertain, complex, and ambiguous world we are living in…but I will. At the risk of preaching to the converted and because you are interested enough to be reading this right now, you know that this is a time of chaos presenting us with great catastrophe and great opportunity. With most institutions failing us as extrinsic sources of wisdom, we need to rediscover and relearn that intrinsic source of wisdom which we all possess but may not know how to activate. Peter's book can help you.

With plenty of life examples growing up in Papua New Guinea and having worked as an actor, a naturopath, a psychologist, a senior organisational coach and facilitator for multinational corporations in many parts of the world, Peter brings a sharp intellect, curious mind, and humble attitude to the exploration and practice of wisdom. Building on the work of Nobel Prize Winner Daniel Kahneman and others, Peter points beyond System 1 and System 2 thinking to a third, more balanced way of thinking. System 3 thinking is balanced, integrated and a more powerful way to deal with the wicked, adaptive challenges we face. The Greek philosopher Aristotle said that wisdom begins from seeing things from at least three perspectives. Peter discusses the risks of a binary approach to problem solving which is a quantum jump beyond the familiar, 'It's my way or the highway' unilateral approach. He gives contemporary examples based on how Australia and other governments are dealing with the global pandemic to illustrate the shortcomings of limiting ourselves to just system 1 and system 2 thinking.

This book is more than just another 'how to' book that you can use as a leader, coach, OD change agent, and the like. It is an invitation to reflect on your own decision-making processes and cognitive biases. We have learned from quantum physics and hard-earned experience that no one stands outside the system once you have observed it. We are all part of many systems and our state of consciousness affects those around us in ways that we are just beginning to understand. That's why I highly recommend you take the System 3 profile before reading the book. It will help you become aware of your own ability to make wise decisions based on the criteria Peter has discovered. I discovered my own growing edge in making wiser decisions. It is in the area of Decisiveness. Peter suggests, 'If you can make a positive difference in another's life or in a community, then take action. Don't delay...Be known for your position.' That got me right between the eyes. Although this book explores the effects of social media on our decision-making ability, it got me thinking about the best ways of making my position known... and it's not necessarily on Twitter, Facebook or Instagram.

Sir John Whitmore is considered in the corporate coaching community to be one of the foundational thinkers and promoters of executive coaching. He told me at a conference that we were both speaking at that the reason many Mafia-like groups moved in after the dissolution of the old Soviet Union was because people under the old regime did not know how to think for themselves. He said that he saw executive coaching as a way of teaching people how to think for themselves. Socrates said something like 'I can't teach you anything except how to think'. Peter is continuing in this great tradition. That is why I am highly recommending you read this book... for yourself, for the organisations you work with, and for the world.

John Matthews
Director
Illumined

Introduction
Moments of choice

I heard the roaring sound of the river before I could see it, rising up through the moss-laden jungle of the ravine. It was still raining as we carefully picked our way down a steep and slippery trail.

I was in the Eastern Highlands of Papua New Guinea in 1968. I was 14 years old. My friend from boarding school and his father, a tea plantation owner, were ahead of me. We arrived at the bank of what looked like a horizontal waterfall, seething brown and angry through the dark, dense foliage. This was day three of a seven-day patrol for the Department of Agriculture, Stock, and Fisheries from Garaina across the Owen Stanley Ranges to the gold-mining town of Wau. I overheard a local villager tell one of our bearers they had lost a bull in the river a few days before. They found pieces of it several kilometres downstream. The only crossing was a precarious-looking 'bridge': saplings roped together with tree vines. The bearers crossed first, carrying heavy supplies, dancing over the saplings with practised ease. Then my friend and his father, less elegant but confident.

Now it was my turn.

I held on to a single overhead vine for balance and stepped out. The wet and slippery saplings shifted under my weight. Looking down at the water surging under my feet caused me to compensate by leaning upstream. I almost lost balance. Then somehow I was half way across. But my overhead vine was now out of reach. Suddenly, one of the saplings twisted and I slipped and fell, desperately reaching for a hold. I found myself straddling the bridge as it quivered with the shock of my fall, rocking from side to side. The roar of the river pounded in my ears. Rain and tears blinded me. I was stuck. I couldn't turn around and go back. And the saplings were too wet and uncertain to try to go forward. Yet, I knew this was the only way across. I clung to the slippery wood over a raging torrent in a nameless valley in the middle of a lost world, terrified.

My friend's father called out to me. 'You're okay!' he said. 'You're nearly there. Don't look down, look at me, and move forward one arm at a time'. I looked at him and tried moving my arms. I found I could pull myself forward, even as the saplings twisted and bent under my body. Slowly, I made progress. 'Keep going, you're doing great,' my friend's father encouraged. 'Look at me, you can do it.' The bridge swayed and flexed. It was like gripping onto some sort of wild animal which was trying to throw me. 'Almost there now – keep looking at me.' And then I was on the other side, collapsing onto the muddy bank with tears of fear and exhaustion.

That was the genesis for this book … although I didn't know it at the time. I had to cross quite a few slippery bridges over raging rivers before I sensed there was a pattern in how I made choices in life. And then it took me a long period of trial and error to figure out the difference between choosing wisely and choosing foolishly.

Perhaps you feel like you're stuck on a 'bridge' at the moment: the way back is just as uncertain as the way forward; you've run out of options; what you know isn't enough; there's no one to turn to for advice; and the consequences of getting it wrong could be disastrous.

What should you do?

CROSSING BRIDGES

I grew up in the regional town of Lae, Papua New Guinea with my family. My father was an airline pilot. Once we reached high-school age my sister and I were shipped off to boarding school in Brisbane, Australia. When I finished high school I worked for a year in Lae and then moved to Brisbane with my family. I completed a Bachelor of Economics Degree at the University of Queensland and then took an Honours year in Organisational Psychology. My first job was working as an organisational psychologist for a start-up nickel mining venture in the heart of the Great Victoria Desert, Western Australia. Then I transferred to one of the joint venture partners in Mount Isa, outback Queensland.

My girlfriend at the time got me involved in amateur theatre. Then she told me she wanted to go on the road with a travelling theatre company. It was a 'bridge' moment. Should I follow my heart, abandon my career and join her? Or should I follow my head and let her go? I chose to follow my heart. It turned out to be foolish in the short term, but in the long term my girlfriend became my wife and I resumed my career in Brisbane working as an organisational psychologist for the state electricity authority.

While we were travelling through Far North Queensland I had become intrigued with natural medicine. I took up part-time study, and topped biochemistry in my first year despite failing high school chemistry, twice. I was offered a paid apprenticeship working for a clinic of alternative medicine in the regional city of Toowoomba, two hours' drive west of Brisbane.

Should I take the offer in pursuit of my dream? Or should I maintain my current career? We also had a newborn baby to consider. The wise choice was to reject the offer, turn around and go back across the 'bridge' to the safety of what was known. But I took the offer and moved my family to an unknown city. It was a rocky path. It certainly felt foolish for a long time.

But I had crossed the bridge to a new land. There was no turning back. In the end I graduated with a Bachelor of Naturopathy and a Post-Graduate Diploma of Nutrition. Over many years I set up practices of naturopathic medicine and psychological counselling in South East Queensland, from Noosa to the Gold Coast. I taught clinical subjects at major natural medicine colleges. And I worked in professional services and sales management for some of Australia's biggest natural medicine manufacturers and their North American affiliates. After nearly 20 years in naturopathic clinical practice and education, I was proud to be nominated as one of the pioneers of Functional Medicine in Australia in 2000.

I had crossed a few bridges to get there. But the bridge of my marriage collapsed and threw me into the raging torrent. I was unprepared for the emotional pain of losing my family. It was sink or swim. Should I let myself drown in shame? Or should I swim to the other side, never to return? I reflected on all the choices I had made to arrive at that moment in my life. I recognised my tendency to cross any bridge offered to me. I had always believed that life would be better on the other side. But sometimes it wasn't. I began to question why some of my choices were terrible in the short term but beneficial in the long term, and vice versa.

How could I stop justifying and rationalising my choices?

Who says what a wise choice is anyway?

I resolved to find a better way of thinking about my moments of choice.

THE DISCOVERY OF SYSTEM 3 THINKING

In 2000 I was admitted into the world's first post-graduate university degree in coaching. It was a bridge to a new profession. By the time I graduated from the University of Sydney with a Master's Degree in Applied Science (Coaching Psychology) in 2005, I had developed a portfolio career in executive coaching and training. But I was searching for a different way of thinking about the pain of choice. Then I came across the psychology of wisdom while researching for a paper I delivered at the first Australian Evidence-Based Coaching Conference.

I immersed myself in the psychology of wisdom and wondered how it might be possible to predict a wise choice. What's going on between your ears in that moment of choice? With my background in naturopathic clinical medicine, I was curious about the neuropsychological processes that underpinned decision-making. I presented my ideas in numerous conferences, papers, and book chapters, and formulated decision-making frameworks to help my executive coaching clients make better decisions. In 2007 I ran the first of many 'coaching for wisdom' workshops for colleagues and clients.

Then the global recession of 2008–09 rolled in. I knew the best strategy in a recession is to plant seeds. In 2010 one of those seeds flourished when I began working with my colleague Dr Barry Partridge to develop a measure of decision-making. We won a government technology grant through the University of

Wollongong and we spent the next five years constructing and validating the Decision Processing Survey (DPS). The idea of a third system of thinking emerged from this research. We confirmed Daniel Kahneman's system 1 (intuition and experience) and system 2 (reason and logic) thinking, but we were able to identify a third factor which was statistically different.

Could Kahneman be wrong?

We weren't about to contradict a Nobel Prize winner without good evidence.

Barry and I designed and conducted workshops in decision-making to test our theories. We came to realise just how domain-specific good decision-making is. You learn how to make good decisions at work through training and experience. Making decisions as a firefighter is different to making decisions as a currency trader, or an airline pilot. You rely on a combination of system 1 and system 2 thinking specific to your field of operation.

But we wondered how people made decisions in unpredictable situations: when there's no standard operating procedure; when the impacts of a decision are too complex to predict; or when the effects on people and communities are morally questionable. This is where we theorised that a third system of thinking would be needed. But what, exactly, were the components of this type of thinking?

In 2016, I accepted the role of Director, Research and Curriculum for ICLIF (International Centre for Leadership In Finance), an executive education centre based in Kuala Lumpur, Malaysia. Over three years I ran executive education programs and presented my ideas on 'wise decision-making' to business audiences across South East Asia, Africa, and Europe with support from my colleagues Michael Kossler and Dr Thun Thamrongnawasawat. In mid-2019 I ran a four-day residential program on leadership decision-making for central bankers in Seoul, South Korea. That's where all the ideas about system 3 thinking came together. I even co-designed an online decision-making simulation with UK-based company, Ososim. I figured if system 3 thinking could help hard-bitten bankers from nine different countries in South East Asia make wise choices, it could probably work for just about anybody.

WHAT'S IN THIS BOOK?

Now I finally understood why I had made so many foolish choices in my life, and what I could have done to make it better. If only I had access to the resources I'm sharing with you in this book, I might have changed the course of my life for the better.

My discovery of system 3 thinking presents a unique set of dimensions for choosing wisely. You can take the T3 profile assessment in this book (chapter 2) to find out how well you use system 3 thinking in your decision-making.

I'll show you how you can enhance your own system 3 thinking (chapter 3). And I'll share with you some recent examples of moments of choice in business, government, and personal life, and how they could have turned out differently if the decision-makers had applied system 3 thinking (chapter 4).

I'll also take you through the WISE Framework – a practical tool for working with system 3 thinking when the standard decision-making models don't fit (chapter 5). And I'll show you how you can live a meaningful life and make a positive difference in the world by choosing wisely (chapter 6).

WHAT'S COMING UP?

It's true that we tend to see ourselves as naturally good decision-makers. You will always consider yourself a good parent, a good grandparent, a good driver. We see ourselves through the lens of self-attribution bias as being much better at things than other people are. So, you might ask, *why should I even think about my decision-making? I'm already a good decision-maker, I don't need to learn how to do it.* But knowledge of your decision-making approaches is a prelude to improving your capability to make more effective decisions. You need to know what stops you from making a wise choice, which includes the tendency to jump to conclusions. You think you know what the problem is without really seeing the problem.

In the next chapter, I'm going to show you how bias is both a good and a bad thing, and how to avoid the most common biases, logical fallacies, and heuristics that lead to poor choices.

How your choices get hijacked

Every decision you make is affected by bias. Even believing you are unaffected by bias is itself a bias. But there are ways to solve problems without jumping to conclusions. This chapter shows you how to stay on the lookout for bias, and how you can develop your critical thinking.

EVERYONE IS BIASED EXCEPT ME

I had made a mistake – a big, *huge* mistake. It was the early hours of Valentine's Day, 14 February 2014. I was sitting up with my wife, and tearfully admitting that the two-year consulting partnership with my colleague had been a failure. It was probably an unwise decision to go into the partnership in the first place. 'I told you so,' she said. Worse, I realised I had been duped by my own biases. And as a psychologist I was supposed to know about that stuff. After all,

I had made a study of bias and logical fallacy. Bias happened to *other people*.

A week earlier, I had questioned my business partner about her excessive use of our joint resources to build her own programs. Why did she need to travel to the US to attend more courses at our expense? She went anyway. And while she was away, I investigated why our business was collapsing, and why I hadn't seen it.

Upon examination, I discovered our business model had been flawed from the outset. I hadn't seen this because I had fallen for four common human biases:

- We never could quite agree on what the business was for. The *self-serving bias* is the tendency to seek out information that advances your own self-interests. I was unknowingly focused on how much revenue I had brought into the business and how much this supported my own ego. In fact, I had delivered more paid hours than my business partner, yet her passion, energy, and focus were clearly dedicated to her own programs. In effect, our business had provided funding and support to help her build her profile, but at the expense of the partnership.

- We never consistently got our marketing together. We were sending different marketing messages to the same audience. I realised I had let myself be led by *confirmation bias*: the wishful thinking for something to be true so that you only see information which confirms it. I was focused on what I chose to see that was good about the business and not on what wasn't working. In the end, it was all too late. We had squandered the opportunities we had in the first year.

- I also became aware of how my business partner had been running our partnership as her own company by default.

She had co-opted her friends and colleagues to work for her in cosy, yet costly arrangements. I hadn't exercised the kind of managerial oversight I should have because I had been deceived by *cognitive fluency* – the ease with which you process information to generate an understanding of what that information means. Her soothing assurances all sounded good.

- Yet, I also realised that I had allowed this all to happen. I hadn't been willing to let go of the partnership even when my business partner began hinting before Christmas that we might have to go our separate ways if things didn't improve. Even when she announced on 3 February that this was a make-or-break quarter, I refused to accept it because of *sunk cost fallacy* – the bias to continue a behaviour or endeavour as a result of previously invested resources (time, money, or effort). I saw the partnership as a path to long-term prosperity. And after investing so much I couldn't just walk away.

I became surprised, then angry, and then furious by what had been happening. I met with my business partner on 27 February as soon as she got back from her course in the US. I closed the door and announced that I was winding up the business. I had a deed of agreement drawn up which enabled us to deliver remaining con-tracts and distribute all assets and liabilities. In the end we parted amicably. But – like so many others – I had paid a high price for the real-world effects of cognitive bias and logical fallacy.

JUMPING TO CONCLUSIONS

We jump to conclusions based on our experience or 'gut feeling'. It's very easy to do that, but it's not necessarily the best way to make a decision when you're not sure which way to go. Your gut feeling may sound very nice, but there are enormous biases in gut feelings. You have to be careful to protect against them. Take the time to see the problem first. Step back and ask yourself:

- What is the problem?
- Who shares the problem?
- Where is the problem leading me?
- What are my options?

American neuroscientist and adjunct professor at Stanford University David Eagleman points out in his 2011 book *Incognito: The secret lives of the brain* that the human brain has evolved to solve problems that are mostly social in nature, but it's not so good at logic. When we came together as early hominid groups on the plains of East Africa, we survived by banding together and hunting together. Our social wiring has come from that early evolution. We tend to be quite good at sensing social situations and solving those problems.

But logic wasn't necessary then. You didn't have to sit down and think logically about whether that rustle in the undergrowth was a sabre-toothed tiger or just the wind. You instinctively knew that you had to run, or you had to attack. Fight or flight is still a factor today in your decision-making.

Heuristics, logical fallacies, and cognitive biases have all evolved as shortcuts to thinking because of the way our social decision-making has evolved.

Let's take a look at each of these.

Heuristics

A heuristic is a mental shortcut that allows you to solve problems and make judgments quickly and efficiently. It's a 'rule-of-thumb' strategy. For example:

- You walk into a boardroom for the first time, and you size up the people seated around the table. You make a decision that the woman sitting at the far end of the table can't possibly be of any influence because she's too short. And you pay more attention to the guy sitting on your right because he's wearing a smartly cut suit. Heuristics allow you to navigate your way in social situations with such ready shortcuts. But they could easily lead you astray: it turns out the woman you thought was too short is the CEO, and the guy in the smart suit is the lawyer who has been sent in to wind up the company.

- The *availability heuristic* explains why you tend to overestimate your likelihood of dying in a dramatic event such as a plane crash or an act of terrorism. Dramatic, violent deaths are usually more highly publicised and are therefore more available to you from recent memory. Common but mundane events are hard to bring to mind, so you tend to underestimate them. These include deaths from suicides, strokes, and diabetes. It's one of the reasons why you're more easily swayed by a single, vivid story than by a large body of statistical evidence. It's a survival heuristic, but it's not very accurate.

- You value your possessions according to the amount of effort you put into acquiring them or building them. This is called the *effort heuristic*. This causes you to hold on to assets which cost a lot of energy. It's a survival strategy. This explains why you're surprised when you list for sale something which you treasure and get a ridiculous offer from a buyer who doesn't see it as quite so valuable.

Logical fallacies

Logical fallacies are the threads of arguments you have in your mind that stem from a logical error. For example:

- Presuming that a real or perceived relationship between things means that one is the cause of the other. For example, global temperatures have been rising over the past few centuries, while at the same time the number of pirates has been decreasing. Therefore, pirates cool the world and global warming is a hoax.

- Judging something good or bad on the basis of where it comes from, or from whom it comes. For example, after being accused of lying in a cable news interview, the politician said that we should all be very wary of the things we hear on the media, because we all know it's fake news.

- Saying the burden of proof lies not with a person making a claim, but with someone else who is trying to disprove the claim. For example, a conspiracy theorist declaring that a particular politician is taking bribes. No one can prove that the politician isn't taking bribes, so the conspiracy theorist thinks his claim is a valid one.

Bias

You think you're logical, but you're not – according to journalist David McRaney in his 2012 book *You Are Not So Smart*. It's true that you can reach a good conclusion without all the facts. You can fill in the blanks. Human beings are very good at that. But cognitive biases are baked into your DNA. They are predictable patterns of thought and behaviour that lead you to draw not-so-smart conclusions.

For example:

- In the *belief bias*, if a conclusion supports your existing beliefs, you'll rationalise anything that supports this conclusion. You'll look for and find evidence to support your beliefs and ignore anything that contradicts them, so you are perpetually reinforced. You become impervious to criticism.

- In the *anchoring bias*, the first thing you judge influences your judgement of all that follows. For example, is the population of Vietnam greater than 40 million? Without Googling it, what's your best estimate of Vietnam's population? Predictably, your estimate will be around 10% above or below 40 million. But the actual population of Vietnam is 97 million (as of April 2020). The reason why your estimate was probably inaccurate is because you 'anchored' on the first available piece of information: 40 million.

- The bias of *loss aversion* explains why you feel the pain of loss more keenly than the pleasure of gain. It's a survival instinct to fear losing what you have: food, money, possessions. It's why something bad happening attracts your attention more than something good. For example, supposing you are an insurance assessor and you've just been notified that three vessels sank off the local port yesterday (must have been a stormy day), and each vessel holds cargo worth $200,000 which will be lost if not salvaged within 12 hours. Your job is to recover as much cargo as possible. You approach a salvage company and they give you two options, both of which cost the same. Option A will save the cargo of one of the three vessels worth $200,000.

Option B has a one-third probability of saving the cargo on all three vessels, worth $600,000, but a two-third probability of saving nothing. Which option will you choose, A or B? You will likely choose option A because at least you know you'll get something back, whereas option B has a two-thirds probability of losing everything. But in terms of assessing the numbers, both option A and option B essentially achieve the same outcome. You can do the math. But option B feels like you might lose more. And human beings will do almost anything to avoid the emotional pain of loss.

Cognitive biases do save your brain time and energy through mental shortcuts. But they are just tools: useful in the right contexts, but harmful in others. Karl Popper, eminent philosopher of science and author of the 1999 book *All Life Is Solving Problems*, said, 'If we're uncritical, we shall always find what we want. We shall look for and find confirmations and we'll look away from and not see whatever might be dangerous to our pet theories.' In other words, you tend to find what you're looking for.

First, put up the set

For a while in 1978, I was an actor with the Owl and the Pussycat touring theatre company. We travelled through the outback towns and coastal cities of Far North Queensland staging plays and musicals. Our marketing hook was to serve free beer for an hour before the show: 'We've stopped for one night! And we'd like to buy the whole town drinks, so bring everyone along. Be assured this is a full stage show. All jugs of beer and all wine served for one hour before this production are free!' To pull this off we had to stage our productions in the lounge bar of the local pub. And we had to convince the publican to give us a keg of beer and a couple of cases of wine in return for a share of the ticket price. Initially, most publicans were sceptical. 'Tell you what,' we'd say. 'We'll set up the stage so you can see what we're offering, and if you don't like it, we'll take it down and be on our way.'

It would take about an hour to completely assemble the pre-decorated proscenium, lights, stage, and backdrops complete with doors and windows. When assembled we would turn on the lights and invite the publican to take a look. Few of them had seen a stage show before. And this looked like a full movie set in their own local bar. Without realising it at the time, we were exploiting the anchoring bias.

Once the publican was anchored on the visual presence of the show, they would fall over backwards and offer us as many kegs as we wanted.

I've found it to be as true in life as it is in showbusiness; if you want to convince someone, first put up the set. Anchor them on the first impression. Show 'em what you've got.

You're either with me or against me

I was in the main ballroom of the Sheraton Mirage Hotel on the Gold Coast, Queensland with 400 healthcare practitioners, many of them friends and colleagues. They were gathered for the first Australian Vitality and Longevity Assessment program in late May 1998. And the spotlight was on me as the key presenter. The company hosting the program had sent me to California two months earlier as part of a collaboration with the founders of the program.

Yet now my manager had taken over and he was droning on in his inimitable style. He was losing the audience. I was seething. It was up to me to honour the design integrity of the program, and here was my manager changing it at will. That night I confronted him. Either get with the program or get out of the way, I said. It was a career-limiting move. Shortly after the program I was asked to leave the company on a pretext. At the time I felt I was standing up for principles, ideals, and even higher consciousness. I saw myself as a knight fighting a noble quest.

Yet I was blinded by my own belief bias that I alone knew what was best for the program. I rationalised my actions as right versus wrong. Years later, I met up with my manager who apologised to me for his overreaction. And I apologised for my intransigence. We had cornered each other with no room for stepping down. I wondered if the situation needed to play out in the way it did for both of us to let go of our biases and grow.

THE EFFECT OF SOCIAL MEDIA

The human brain is lazy. It likes fast and simple because thinking consumes energy. After millennia of evolution, we are configured to jump to conclusions. Which is why we have developed hundreds of shortcuts, predictions, assumptions, and hacks. For example, the 'Google Effect' is the tendency to forget information that can be found readily online. Why bother remembering things that you can instantly look up on your device? Even managing your important personal information can be outsourced, thus freeing up memory storage space in the brain. A survey by Kaspersky Lab in 2015 found around 90% of people use the internet, and 40% of people use their smartphones to remember personal details.

Your devices have the same conditioning effect as poker machines. They keep you hooked by sending intermittent variable rewards. That's how the algorithms draw you in. Your fear of missing out becomes an addiction. Your social approval is primed by how many tags and likes you get. The need to reciprocate social gestures is exploited to keep you on the platform for a longer period. Message interruption is an effective way of capturing your attention because you notice something that's new and different. This is all bias.

Your biases can easily be exploited for commercial, political, or just plain nasty ends. Social media and online platforms are driven by algorithms which seek to give you more of what you're interested in. Which is fine if you're interested in ponies, or shoes, or holidays. The algorithms will direct you to whole ecosystems of related information. Ponies will connect you to feed lot providers, saddle-makers, gift shops, sellers, and buyers. But if you keep going, the algorithms will connect bridles and harnesses to leather products, bikie clubs, guns, insurrection, and conspiracy theories. It's easy to get lost down the rabbit hole of information. And it's always easier to subscribe than it is to unsubscribe to anything.

What was once the exciting new world of online consumerism, business, and social networking has become a dark ocean of strange creatures with a life of their own. AI permeates every online contact we have. Not AI (Artificial Intelligence), but rather AI (Artificial Ignorance). The algorithms are dumb. They are like viruses which feed on your cognitive biases.

We've got so many people using the internet now – about 3.2 billion users in 2020 – that the way in which the algorithms are written means you can sometimes get great advice and information, but sometimes they can actually lead you into the dark side. If you're looking for advice about depression, they might lead you down the path of how to kill yourself. When people are on the internet, they feel disinhibited and able to say whatever they want because they're not being personally identified. That's quite terrifying. And it's seeping from our smartphones into every aspect of our life. Women experience high levels of abuse, online and in real life. Trolling has been steadily increasing, and this has very real impacts on mental health. People commit suicide because of online trolling.

How to avoid the traps of social media

Professor of Human Development at Cornell University, Robert Sternberg, developed a curriculum for teaching wisdom to a sample of US middle-school students in 2001. His approach is equally valid now to help you recognise the importance of inoculating yourself against the pressures of unbalanced self-interest and small-group interest, and to build your immunity to the viruses of AI (Artificial Ignorance).

In assessing the information-stream you're looking at, ask yourself these questions before you jump to conclusions:

- Whose interests are being served by whatever you're reading or seeing? Who is behind it, and what do they stand to gain from you? Who are the principal sponsors and backers? How are their needs being met by you connecting with them? Follow the money.

- What are my own interests and how are they best served in relation to what I'm reading or seeing? How are my needs for *consistency*, *meaning*, and *acceptance* being met without distortion?

- Recognise the 'means' by which the end is obtained matters, not just the end. Emphasise your own critical, creative, and practical thinking in the service of ends that benefit not only you but others as well. Think how almost everything you consume on social media might be used for better or worse ends, and realise that the ends to which knowledge is put *do* matter.

- Realise that you have three options when you see something online:

  - accept the information without question.

  - filter the information for what seems reasonable or unreasonable.

  - reject the platform, community, or opinion stream – unsubscribe, unfollow, delete.

- How does this information align with my own values? What are my values in relation to this information? Am I being force-fed a set of values that I don't fully subscribe to?

- Think dialectically, realising that both questions and their answers evolve over time, and that the answer to an important life question can differ at different times in your life (such as whether to go to college). Nothing is as fixed or as black and white as you might be led to believe.

- Engage in dialogical thinking, seeking to understand significant problems from multiple points of view. Think how others could see things in a way that is quite different from your own. Try walking a mile in someone else's moccasins. Imagine what it might feel like from their side.

- Search for and then try to reach the *common good* where everyone wins, not just those with whom you identify.

CONCLUSION

Because bias is mostly subconscious, it might simply present as the way you commonly think about a problem. That's just the well-worn train tracks that you go down every time you're in a moment of choice. Yet thinking about your thinking can prepare you to respond more flexibly to the nature of doubt, dilemma, and disruption.

The whole point about this chapter is to help you to see the *Matrix*, to help you see through it, and to be able to make clear decisions that have a positive benefit for more people. I want you to see and navigate the algorithms and avoid the negative influence of AI (Artificial Ignorance).

WHAT'S COMING UP?

In the next chapter, I look at the two systems of thinking you use when trying to solve problems, and introduce you to a third system. My analysis of system 3 thinking, the subject of years of original research on my part, can be harnessed when facing intractable problems.

System 3 thinking explained

Thinking, fast and slow, is how you make most decisions in life. But when uncertainty is high and the consequences are serious, you need a third system of thinking.

'HOW COULD PEOPLE BE SO FOOLISH?'

In late June 2016, I was at the historic Landgut Stober Hotel near the medieval town of Nauen, about an hour-and-a-half's drive west of Berlin, Germany. I was attending the five-day Presencing Foundation Program with Otto Scharmer, senior lecturer at MIT's Sloan School of Management, his team, and 80 participants from around the world. The program followed Otto's 2013 book *Leading from the Emerging Future: From ego-system to eco-system*.

Over four days we participated in Otto's 'theory-U' and the practice of social change methodology, from dialectics to social presencing theatre. Our last night together was a celebration of becoming 'farmers of the social field'. We represented 20 countries dancing in the warm midsummer evening by the shores of lake Groß Behnitz. The next morning came the announcement that Britain had voted to leave the European Union. Prime Minister David Cameron announced his immediate resignation. My European friends were inconsolable, weeping into their muesli over breakfast. Everything we had been learning about the quality of our intention and our attention shaping the world around us appeared to unravel before our eyes.

At that time the consequences of the decision for Europe and geopolitics seemed stark. 'How could people be so foolish?' we lamented. It was the last day of the program. So, we appealed to Otto for some kind of explanation. 'You need to turn towards the problem you see,' he said. 'You have to engage with reality. This is most significant when you face the moment of disruption. Disruption happens. You have no control.' He then explained the causes and conditions for the Brexit decision and explained the destructive effects of the 'inverted-U' process. 'Everything is a cycle of creation and destruction,' he explained. 'Co-sensing is the alpha and the omega. It is everything.' We could see the long cycles of history extending back over thousands of years of human history, and on into the future for thousands more. 'Get out of your bubble,' Otto finally affirmed. 'Put yourself in places where the universe will find you.' I realised at that moment that this is all about sensing the systemic changes from both inside and outside the system. To do that requires a different system of thinking. That's what this chapter is about.

THE MYTH OF RATIONALITY

The Athenian philosopher Plato (427–347 BCE) famously characterised the process of decision-making as being like a charioteer in charge of two horses. One is steady and true and the other is unruly and impulsive. To effectively steer your mind, he wrote, you need to focus on reason and avoid the unruliness of emotion.

Sound familiar? It should, because Plato still sits in most board rooms and executive suites today. Blame Plato for the over-representation of 'male reasoning' versus 'female emotion'. Trust the numbers and don't let your feelings get in the way. After all, it's just business.

Likewise, the founder of psychoanalysis, Sigmund Freud (1856–1939), separated the conscious mind from the deep and emotional abyss of the unconscious mind. It's all your mother's fault, and any success in life is just you trying to keep abreast of her expectations. And a good reason why you should trust your conscious thinking and distrust the weird and wacky unconscious. Keep all that repressed emotion to yourself, thank you very much.

The point is that you've come to expect two sides to your decision-making: the rational and the emotional. And right through primary school, high school, and university you've been trained in rational methods of decision-making and taught to be suspicious of making decisions with your emotions.

The myth of rationality was busted by Seymour Epstein (1924–2016), professor emeritus of psychology at the University of Massachusetts Amherst. He wrote a ground-breaking paper in 1973 titled, 'The Self-Concept Revisited, or a Theory of a Theory'. Epstein argued against Freud's irrational and aggressive unconscious. Far from needing to be controlled or supressed, our most primitive emotional experiences are essential to becoming a fully integrated human being, he said. Epstein developed CEST (Cognitive Experiential Self Theory) to support the idea that both experiential thinking and rational thinking are necessary for personal growth and creativity. He assumed the existence of two parallel, interacting modes of information processing: a rational system and an emotionally driven experiential system. Here at last was confirmation that we rely on both rationality and emotion to make effective decisions. Plato needed both horses after all.

This has become known as the 'dual process theory' of decision-making. You utilise two systems of thinking about a problem: an *intuitive-experiential* style which is automatic, effortless, fast, based on immediate 'gut feeling', and essentially preconscious; and an *analytical-rational* style which is intentional, effortful, logical, reason-oriented, slower and more deliberate, and experienced actively and consciously.

There are individual differences. You might be prone to rely more on an intuitive thinking style for example, and solve problems using your experience of what feels right. Or you might naturally favour a more rational thinking style and lean towards data and analysis, even for the same problem.

This was later popularised by Daniel Kahneman, professor emeritus at Princeton University's Department of Psychology and Woodrow Wilson School of Public and International Affairs, who was awarded the Nobel Prize in 2002 for establishing the field of behavioural economics. Kahneman refers to the intuitive-experiential style as system 1 ('thinking, fast'), and the analytical-rational style as system 2 ('thinking, slow').

Neither system is better than the other. It seems you can readily move between system 1 and system 2 thinking depending on the context and various cues in the environment. Sometimes you engage both systems within the same problem. For example, if the problem is which brand of laundry detergent you should buy, you're more likely to use system 1: 'Well, I've bought that brand before, I'm going to buy it again.' You don't think. You just pick it up and put it in the shopping trolley. If you have to stop and read the label and try to figure out the differences between brands, you're using system 2 to determine your choice.

For bigger decisions, you get a gut feeling: 'That's the house for me.' It can be an overwhelming sense of 'rightness'. You just know that you know. System 1 thinking can be quite powerful. But then you step back and realise you'd better figure out whether you can afford it or not. Then you bring in system 2 thinking to justify to the bank why they should lend you so much money to buy that house.

Most of your decisions are quick, intuitive, and largely sub-conscious. You don't actually think about it too much. You just go by 'what feels right'. Actually, it's hard work to be rational and look at the facts. It takes a lot of energy to analyse things and you're most likely to avoid it if you can. System 2 thinking only kicks in when you need to sit down with a spreadsheet or do some calculations.

But what happens when there isn't enough information to go on and you have to make a really important decision that will likely affect the course of your life and the lives of others?

WISE DECISION-MAKING

Stay or go?

Winter is the best time of year in outback North-West Queensland. Daytime is warm beneath the big desert sky. Temperatures drop sharply at night under the Southern Cross, clear and bright. We had been living in the inland mining city of Mount Isa for four months, and I was two years into my promising career as an organ-isational psychologist and corporate personnel training officer. I was 24. It was early July 1978 when my girlfriend announced that she wanted to join the Owl and the Pussycat theatre company and go on tour.

I had already had my first taste of amateur theatre in Joe Orton's *What the Butler Saw*, a crazy farce set in a mental asylum. I had a bit part that required me to come on stage in only my underpants. We were on stage together again in a big production of the 1950's French musical *Irma La Douce*, with my girlfriend playing the lead role.

She wanted me to go on tour with her. If I put my career first, I would surely lose her. But if I joined her and became a travelling actor, I would forfeit my career. I was stuck on a bridge again. On the day I had to make a decision I left the office and walked around the block trying to weigh up the options. I argued out loud with myself, alternately playing the roles of 'stay' and 'go'. Each time I circled the block I thought I had made up my mind, only to have another doubt enter the conversation. Should I follow my heart or my head? My parents would surely crucify me for going – so would her parents. But we had been together for nearly five years; didn't that count for something? Who was I aiming to please, my parents or my girlfriend? Finally, exhausted, I made up my mind. I went back into the office and prepared my letter of resignation.

In the short term it certainly seemed a foolish decision. Both our parents were indeed shocked, and angry. But now I look back and see the long-term benefits of that decision. I became an actor, which laid the groundwork for my later career as a trainer and facilitator. And I married my girlfriend the following year, which led to four children together over 18 years.

Up or down?

Making a life changing decision is kind of like being on a see-saw. One minute you're up, the next you're down. It's easy to flip between system 1 and system 2 thinking when faced with conflict, just as I did when deciding whether to take to the road with my girlfriend.

Which system of thinking should I have relied on? In the style of the iconic band The Beatles, 'all you need is love' … right? According to Dutch Social Psychologist Ap Dijksterhuis from Radboud University, in Nijmegen, system 1 thinking is all you need when it comes to complex decision-making. In a 2004 study, he showed that unconscious thought led to better decisions in complex conditions than conscious thought.

In a real-world variation of Dijksterhuis's study, my wife and I wanted to buy a new car. After exhaustive research I presented her with a spreadsheet of the top four contenders based on utilisation, fuel consumption, and green star rating. We took each car for a test drive. In the end, we bought the car my wife felt would be best for us. It wasn't even on my list. And it turned out to be the best choice.

Marc Hauser is an American evolutionary biologist and a researcher in primate behaviour, animal cognition, and human behaviour. In his 2006 book *Moral Minds*, he argues that our moral decision-making is hard-wired for immediate 'gut feeling' choices which seek, among other things, the protection of human life. Complex decision-making, including moral reasoning, is a post-facto rationalisation of why you made certain choices. Both system 1 and system 2 thinking seem to be involved in moral judgment, but at different times. In the ultimate irony, Hauser was forced to resign from Harvard University in 2011 when he was found guilty of immorally fabricating data, manipulating experimental results, and publishing falsified results.

Finding wisdom

You might be of the view that wisdom is essentially a spiritual quality and best left to religion and theologies. And yet the quality of your most important decisions can be judged as being more or less wise by others. Other people can always point to your decisions and tell you whether it was foolish or wise.

Wisdom is widely attributed to wise persons. Think about His Holiness the Dalai Lama, for example. You might say, 'Well, he's a wise person. I can't be as wise as that. I can't be the Dalai Lama, so don't ask me to be wise.' Wisdom is supposed to be unattainable by mere mortals. Yet wisdom can be both the property of a person and a function of the condition in which a decision is made.

Research in the psychology of wisdom over the last three decades shows that what constitutes making a wise decision seems to be more than intelligence alone, and more than personality alone. There's some overlap, but the overlap is actually quite small. Wise thinking is a skill, and that skill can be enhanced. You can get better at it. Wise thinking appears to dip in middle age and then goes up. Age is necessary but not a solely sufficient condition for wise decision-making. You can have quite young people exhibiting quite wise behaviour and you can have very foolish baby boomers. Women, however, are somewhat better at wise thinking than men, which should come as no surprise.

Making a wise decision seems to involve both system 1 and system 2 thinking working highly collaboratively. System 2 thinking articulates judgments and makes choices even though it mostly rationalises the ideas and feelings that were generated by system 1. Yet system 2 thinking can also impose more sensible thinking and overrule system 1. One of Kahneman's contributions to decision-making is to characterise the 'personalities' of these two systems of information processing such that they can be more consciously and deliberately applied to everyday choices. To do this requires a kind of meta-understanding.

According to professors of psychology Paul Baltes (1939–2006) from the Max Planck Institute for Human Development and Alex Freund from the University of Zurich (2003), wise decision-making could be more of an 'orchestration' of systems 1 and 2, between what feels right and what is reasonable. Baltes and his colleagues formulated the Berlin Wisdom Paradigm in the 1990s, the first and still the most rigorous measurement of wise decision-making when faced with a dilemma.

When it comes to making a wise decision with your heart (system 1 thinking) or your head (system 2 thinking), it turns out neither system is definitive.

You need a third system of thinking.

THREE HEADS ARE BETTER THAN ONE

At first, I thought it was spam. The message had come through to an old email address that I no longer used. Annoyed, I directed the sender to use my proper address. They did. It was an executive search recruiter from Singapore asking if I would be interested in applying for a job with an agency of the Central Bank of Malaysia. Was this a joke? It still seemed like spam to me. But I decided to reply; 'Sure,' I said.

The recruiter asked for my CV and other documents, and I responded. This was January 2016 and it had been 18 years since

I last had a job, much less applied for one. As an organisational development consultant and an executive coach in my own business I considered myself unemployable. The recruiter contacted me in early February 2016 and arranged a Skype interview with the CEO of the company based in Kuala Lumpur, Malaysia. *Okay, I thought, I'll play along.* I was having my most successful year in business, so I had nothing to lose.

The interview was intriguing and seemed to go surprisingly well. Afterwards I thought, *if they're serious they should fly me up to Kuala Lumpur for a face-to-face meeting.* Business class, of course. And I should stay in a five-star hotel. What the heck, at least I'll get a free international trip.

And they did. I spent the Easter long weekend in March 2016 staying in a five-star hotel in Kuala Lumpur and meeting everyone at ICLIF (International Centre for Leadership In Finance). I was made a conditional offer of employment, and I began to think this might just work.

So, no … it *wasn't* spam.

Waiting for my midnight return flight to Sydney I considered the moment of choice. Was I really capable of this? Did I really want to leave everything behind and move to Malaysia for three years or more? I certainly hadn't been looking for work. How would I manage re-entry to the Sydney market when all my networks would have faded by the time I got back? How would this affect my relationship with my wife, as indeed it must? How would I really feel living alone in a strange city? Was this a once-in-a-lifetime opportunity? How would I feel rejecting it in favour of staying home and playing it safe? Would I regret the decision?

Back home, I began to cool on the idea. I could see the dance between my system 1 and system 2 thinking. But somehow that wasn't enough. The recruiter in Singapore kept pushing for an answer. They were keen to get me onboard, he said. They submitted a generous expat package. But the tax implications meant we would both have to relocate to Kuala Lumpur and declare ourselves ex-residents of Australia. My wife was devastated at the prospect. She didn't want to move away from her friends and support network. How could I make such a selfish decision, which would cause her so much pain? At the same time, I was also negotiating to join the Human Capital Consulting division of Deloitte Australia.

Which path should I take? I was stuck on a bridge again. Should I go, or should I stay? Both scenarios were plausible.

The genesis of system 3 thinking

Instead of squeezing the decision through system 1 and system 2 thinking, I considered the longer-term consequences and benefits to our relationship, to our financial future, and to my own personal and professional development. This was a practical application of system 3 thinking, and quite different to the decision I made to go on the road with a travelling theatre company all those years ago. I was using system 1, system 2, *and* system 3 thinking in a life-changing moment of choice.

I moved to Kuala Lumpur in early July and my wife joined me in late August 2016. It was a rocky road at first. I realised that my decision had caused significant pain and distress for my wife. This was not how I wanted it to be. However, we returned to Australia in early July 2019 at the end of the three-year contract considerably better off than when we left and with rich cultural travel experiences.

Did my decision achieve a common good? My wife credits her ongoing pain and distress to the years living in Malaysia without competent allied health support. Yet, the decision provided magical memories and enabled me to reach the pinnacle of my corporate career. Two heads might be better than one I discovered, but three heads are even better.

THE THIRD SYSTEM OF THINKING

Whenever you read 'neuroscience' in a sentence it bestows an aura of respectability. That's a cognitive bias of course. So, I want to tell you about the neuroscience behind system 3 thinking. It all started with a ground-breaking study of the neurocircuitry of wisdom in 2009. Dr Dilip Jeste, an American geriatric neuropsychiatrist, Director of the Stein Institute for Research in Aging, and his colleagues at the University of California, San Diego School of Medicine, suggested that some areas of the brain inhibit or modulate brain regions involved in emotional processing and response.

For example, participants who completed moral reasoning dilemmas while undergoing fMRI (Functional Magnetic Resonance Imaging), and who showed higher wisdom scores on a psychometric assessment, demonstrated greater engagement of a part of the brain called the DMN (Default Mode Network). This suggests that a third system might be involved in the ability to recognise and process social and emotional cues relevant to wise decision-making. The DMN is normally associated with 'wakeful rest' when daydreaming and 'mind wandering'. But it is now known to contribute to elements of experience, such as when you're thinking about others, thinking about yourself, remembering the past, and planning for the future. The DMN appears to 'orchestrate' both hedonic (pleasure) and eudaimonic (wellbeing) brain states.

It seems highly likely that the DMN is the site of a third system of thinking in the brain. At least the concept is useful to distinguish modes of thinking which are more aligned with choosing wisely than system 1 and system 2 thinking. According to Jeste and his colleagues, this third system of wise thinking involves six components: social advising, emotion regulation, pro-social behaviours, insight, tolerance for divergent values, and decisiveness.

Other researchers have mapped out the characteristics of wise thinking. Professor of Developmental Psychology at Alpen-Adria University Klagenfurt, Austria, Judith Glück and colleagues identified the five criteria of wisdom-related performance drawn from the Berlin Wisdom Paradigm – rich factual knowledge, rich procedural knowledge, lifespan contextualism, value relativism and tolerance, knowledge about handling uncertainty – together with the characteristics of self-transcendence, mindfulness, and compassion.

Associate Professor of psychology and Director of the Wisdom and Research Lab at the University of Waterloo in Ontario, Canada, Igor Grossman and his colleagues have identified four elements of wise thinking: weigh up uncertainty and change, intellectual humility, search for integration and compromise, and engage others' perspectives.

THE SIX DIMENSIONS OF SYSTEM 3 THINKING

Since 2016, I've been exploring the dimensions of system 3 thinking: what makes it different from system 1 and 2 thinking? When do you use it? Does it contribute to wise decision-making?

I constructed a self-assessment questionnaire by combining items from the University of California San Diego Wisdom Scale (SD-WISE) (2017), the Brief Wisdom Screening Scale (BWSS)

(2017) from the Berlin Wisdom Paradigm, and the Situated Wise Reasoning Scale (SWIS) (2017) from the Wisdom and Research Lab at the University of Waterloo in Ontario, Canada. Over three years I collected responses from a wide sample of middle managers and consultants in South East Asia, Europe, and Australia. Initial factor analysis revealed nine dimensions. However, with further refinement and more data I established six validated dimensions of system 3 thinking which are measured by the T3 (system 3 thinking) Profile:

1. **Focus** (questions relating to task attention): being able to attend to a problem and the circumstances, while at the same time paying attention to what's going on around you. It's how well you perceive all the elements of a problem that might be complex and difficult to solve.

2. **Life experience** (questions drawn from self-transcendence and openness to new experience): reflecting on lessons from your own life, and your capacity to tap into the broad panoply of other people's life experience through books, Google, movies, TV streaming content, games, and various social media platforms. You have access to so much information about other people's experiences (real and imaginary) to draw on.

3. **Decisiveness** (questions about readiness to make decisions and readiness to give advice): it seems counterintuitive to wise decision-making but you can't sit on the fence and contemplate for too long. You do have to make decisions, even if it means making lots of quick decisions.

4. **Compassion** (questions about self-compassion and insight): Compassion is a thoughtful response to an injustice, for example. And compassion is also strongly emotional.

When you have strong emotions around compassion you will feel called to respond to those emotions, to do something about it, which is the definition of compassion.

5. **Emotional regulation** (questions about controlling emotions as well as peace of mind): you realise you have a rich emotional life and you're able to recognise and have insight into your emotions, and to use them in making decisions. To use the emotion of frustration or the emotion of unfairness to help you make a decision is quite different to lashing out in anger or frustration at somebody.

6. **Tolerance for divergent values** (questions connected with accepting others' morals and values, insight into the reasons for your own actions, and openness to diverse viewpoints): you identify with your own beliefs, your own value system, but you're also open and curious to the fact that other people think differently and have different value systems to you. And importantly, you can contend with that.

What are the differences between systems 1, 2, and 3 thinking? (See figure overleaf.) The dimensions of system 3 thinking are thoughtful. They're slower. They're considerate. For example, compassion is not an intuitive response, it's a thoughtful response. The difference between feeling sad, angry, or upset about an issue, and then converting those feelings into some practical series of steps that you can take is the difference between empathy and compassion. Empathy can arise quite quickly as part of system 1 thinking, and then empathy can shift into compassion as part of system 3 thinking, because it's a more thoughtful response.

You actually use system 3 thinking rarely. You don't draw on it often because you're mostly using system 1 and sometimes system 2. System 3 thinking kicks in when you really have to stop and step back and say, *I don't know what to do here. I'm out of my depth. I'm at this crossroad and I don't know whether to go left or right* (metaphorically speaking). *I don't have enough information to guide me. And the decision I'm going to make is going to affect, not just me, but other people, and I can't predict what the outcome is going to be.* You'll try to use system 1 thinking to *feel* your way through the problem. And you'll try to *analyse* the information using system 2 thinking. But when you run out of information, that's when you'll benefit from system 3 thinking.

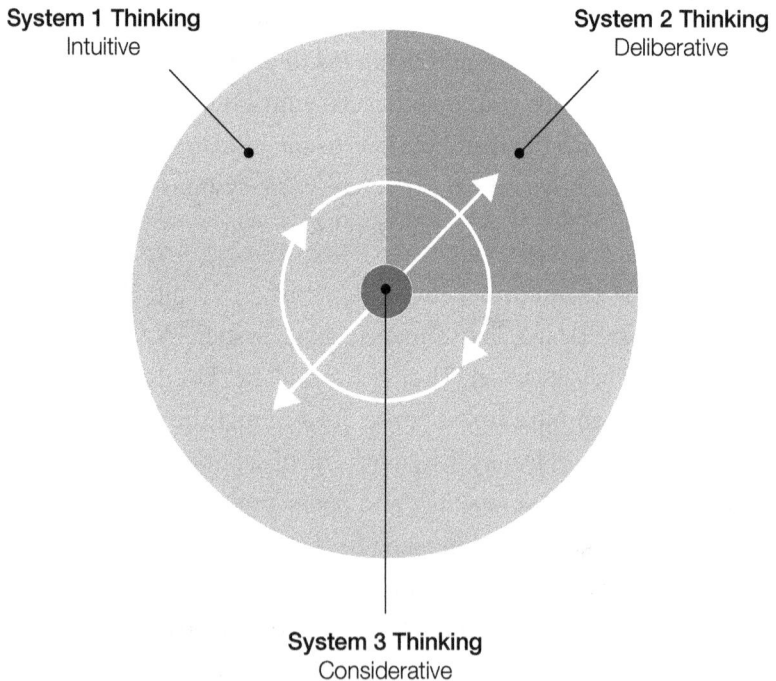

System 1 Thinking
Intuitive

System 2 Thinking
Deliberative

System 3 Thinking
Considerative

System 1 thinking seems more geared to the present moment. By definition it's more of a short-term perspective because it's fairly immediate; it's what you're feeling at the time. System 2 thinking seems to have a lot to do with things which have happened in the past, although when you're making calculations you're thinking about present, past and future. System 3 thinking has both short-term and long-term perspectives to it. Short-term, because you actually have to act decisively; long-term because you're thinking about the ramifications and the consequences of your actions. You're thinking about who this might affect, what the downstream impact might be, both positive and negative. There is more of a longer-term perspective implicit in system 3 thinking.

THE T3 PROFILE

How well are you likely to apply system 3 thinking? The T3 (system 3 thinking) Profile measures your most likely decision-making approaches. Read each of the following statements carefully and tick the box that most honestly describes how you see yourself at the present time in relation to each statement. There are no right or wrong answers. The information from this questionnaire is intended to be helpful for your development.[1]

---

1   Take the T3 profile online here: www.peterjwebb.com.

		Strongly disagree	Disagree	Neither disagree nor agree	Agree	Strongly agree
1.	I tend to postpone making major decisions for as long as I can.	☐ 5	☐ 4	☐ 3	☐ 2	☐ 1
2.	My heart goes out to people who are unhappy.	☐ 1	☐ 2	☐ 3	☐ 4	☐ 5
3.	I am okay with others having morals and values other than my own.	☐ 1	☐ 2	☐ 3	☐ 4	☐ 5
4.	I cannot filter my negative emotions.	☐ 5	☐ 4	☐ 3	☐ 2	☐ 1
5.	I enjoy being exposed to viewpoints different from my own.	☐ 1	☐ 2	☐ 3	☐ 4	☐ 5
6.	When I'm doing a task, I focus all my attention on that task.	☐ 1	☐ 2	☐ 3	☐ 4	☐ 5
7.	I always recover well from emotional stress.	☐ 1	☐ 2	☐ 3	☐ 4	☐ 5
8.	I generally learn something from every person I meet.	☐ 1	☐ 2	☐ 3	☐ 4	☐ 5
9.	I have trouble making decisions.	☐ 5	☐ 4	☐ 3	☐ 2	☐ 1
10.	I take time to reflect on my thoughts.	☐ 1	☐ 2	☐ 3	☐ 4	☐ 5

	Strongly disagree	Disagree	Neither disagree nor agree	Agree	Strongly agree
11. I get completely absorbed in what I'm doing, so that all my attention is focused on it.	☐ 1	☐ 2	☐ 3	☐ 4	☐ 5
12. If I see someone going through a difficult time, I try to be caring toward that person.	☐ 1	☐ 2	☐ 3	☐ 4	☐ 5
13. I am able to make sense of every aspect of my life.	☐ 1	☐ 2	☐ 3	☐ 4	☐ 5
14. I would rather someone else make a decision for me if I am uncertain.	☐ 5	☐ 4	☐ 3	☐ 2	☐ 1
15. It is important that I understand the reasons for my actions.	☐ 1	☐ 2	☐ 3	☐ 4	☐ 5
16. I have trouble thinking clearly when I am upset.	☐ 5	☐ 4	☐ 3	☐ 2	☐ 1
17. I often don't know what to tell people when they come to me for advice.	☐ 5	☐ 4	☐ 3	☐ 2	☐ 1
18. My peace of mind is not easily upset.	☐ 1	☐ 2	☐ 3	☐ 4	☐ 5

Scoring your T3 profile

Your T3 Profile results are referenced against a global database to show whether you're actually high, medium, or low on each of the six dimensions of system 3 thinking. The database is made up of mostly junior to senior level managers across commercial and government organisations. You're being compared to that cohort. You're not being compared to students at universities.

You will notice that each box you ticked in the T3 Profile contains a number. Enter the number for each item you ticked in the table below, then add them together *horizontally* as indicated to get a total in column A for each dimension.

Item no.	Your score	Item no.	Your score	Item no.	Your score	Item no.	Your score	Col. A total	Dimension
6	11							+ =	F
8	13							+ =	L
1	9	14		17				+ =	D
2	10	12						+ =	C
4	7	16		18				+ =	E
3	5	15						+ =	T

Now take your totals from Column A and circle the number where it appears on the chart below for each dimension. This shows how you compare with the global database. You may be high, medium, or low compared with others on each of these dimensions.

Range	F	L	D	C	E	T
High	10	10	20	15	20	15
			19		19	
	9	9	18	14	18	
			17			
Medium	8	8	16	13	17	14
			15	12	16	
	7	7	14	11	15	13
					14	
			13	10	13	
					12	
			12	9	11	
					10	
Low	6	6	11	8	9	12
	5	5	10	7	8	11
	4	4	9	6	7	10
	3	3	8	5	6	9
	2	2	7	4	5	8
			6	3	4	7
			5			6
			4			5
						4
						3

How did you score with your T3 profile? Whether you scored low, medium, or high on each of these dimensions is a good indication of how you're likely to respond when you're faced with real-life doubt or dilemma or disruption, as shown in the following table.

Dimension	High	Medium	Low
F Focus	You are less easily distracted than others and better able to focus your attention on the issue at hand	You focus well on those issues that demand your attention, although sometimes you get distracted	You sometimes find it difficult to maintain focused attention on issues and you are easily distracted
L Life experience	You easily reflect on the successes and failures of your life and on others' biographies and you provide personal advice	You recognise your own life lessons and those from others' biographies and you give advice to others based on rules to live by	You generally avoid giving advice to others about their life problems and prefer to keep your own counsel
D Decisiveness	You consider all the available information, but you are more inclined than others to make quick decisions and move on	You try to consider all the available information, but sometimes you get stuck and delay your decision until you feel more comfortable	You find it difficult to decide even after considering all the available information, preferring to let others make the decision
C Compassion	You care deeply about issues that affect the wellbeing of people in general and you strive to make decisions for the common good	You feel the impact of your decisions on the wellbeing of people in general and you try to balance the interests of all concerned	You are sensitive to the wellbeing of people in general and you try to make decisions that cause the least amount of harm

Dimension	High	Medium	Low
E Emotion regulation	You easily recognise your own emotions when they arise, and you are not readily triggered or provoked by others' reactions	You manage your own emotional state quite well most of the time, although others can 'press your buttons' sometimes and provoke a reaction in you	You acknowledge your emotions, but you are only human, and if others 'press your buttons', you will 'give as good as you get'
T Tolerance for divergent values	You have a broad acceptance of the variation of beliefs, spiritual practices, and values across human communities, and you are not easily offended	You readily acknowledge and accommodate others' beliefs, spiritual practices, and values, provided they don't significantly transgress your own	You recognise the differences in beliefs, spiritual practices, and values in others, but you firmly adhere to your own value system

Most people tend to come up medium across the range and high for one or none of these dimensions. What does that mean? Does that mean somehow that you're incompetent, you're dull, you lack intelligence or compassion, you're not a good human being? Of course not. It doesn't mean any of those things. This is not a measure of your intelligence. It's not a measure of your personality, it's not a measure of your competence, your job performance, or any other element. This is simply a measure of the likelihood that you will use one or more of the dimensions of system 3 thinking when you are faced with doubt, dilemma, or disruption. Someone who scores high on all six dimensions has a higher probability of responding favourably in a situation that is non-predictable and that demands a considered and wise response. Somebody who is low or medium across all six dimensions has not developed strongly enough around those dimensions.

CONCLUSION

There are six dimensions to system 3 thinking:

- **Focus** – pay attention to what really matters.
- **Life experience** – discern what makes common sense.
- **Decisiveness** – try small actions to find out what works best.
- **Compassion** – demonstrate care for humanity through consistent action.
- **Emotional regulation** – use your emotions without feeling overwhelmed.
- **Tolerance for divergent values** – acknowledge different value systems.

You've now learned to distinguish the three systems of thinking:

- System 1 is automatic and fast.
- System 2 is slower, more logical and rational.
- System 3 is more global and holistic, taking into account things that go beyond the pure logic and rationality of the situation, and your own fluttering of emotion.

It's not whether a decision feels right or not; there's a bigger consideration here.

You've scored your T3 Profile, and now you know how you compare to others in terms of the likelihood that you will utilise the six dimensions of system 3 thinking in the future.

There's no guarantee that applying all six dimensions of system 3 thinking at a high level will result in choosing wisely. But if you become practised at applying system 3 thinking you increase the probability of delivering a better decision outcome.

These dimensions are not fixed. They're malleable. You can develop them, you can train for them, you can get better at them. Indeed, training yourself to use these dimensions more effectively should be part of your professional development, because you are going to face problems in the future for which nothing could have prepared you.

WHAT'S COMING UP?

Now you understand what system 3 thinking is and you have some insight into your own strengths, you need to know how to develop those dimensions which appear less developed for you. In the next chapter, I introduce some of the most exciting (and controversial) news in this book: how to improve your wisdom by developing your system 3 thinking! Wise at any age.

How to enhance your system 3 thinking

To choose wisely, use system 3 thinking. This new kind of thinking offers six dimensions. Each is a capability you can develop. They are not fixed dimensions like intelligence. They can be improved. In this chapter you'll learn about each dimension and how you can develop your capability in it.

IT'S ALL ABOUT CHOICES

Langata Women's Prison is the largest female prison in Nairobi, Kenya. It is situated south-west of the city centre, just off the Ngong Forest Road which divides the now fashionable suburb of Langata from Kibera Town, the largest slum in Sub-Saharan Africa. The metal front gate is painted British racing green, a relic of colonial rule in the 1960s. Nothing much has changed since then. Behind the walls, the prison buildings are low set, closely packed concrete hutches scattered across a hillside. I was taking part in the five-day Leader's Quest program in September 2016. We were touring the prison facilities as a guest of the Governor, Madam Olivier, and Theresa and Joss, founders of the charity Clean Start which helps ex-prisoners acclimatise to life outside.

We felt some trepidation being admitted through the infamous green gate. The Governor quickly put us at ease, explaining her philosophy of prisoner rehabilitation and answering all our questions. I asked her, 'How would our visit impact the inmates?' She said, 'Visits such as yours are considered a highlight and everyone prepares for weeks and months in advance.' We were escorted through the prison grounds visiting the wood-fired laundry and kitchen, the market garden, the workshops, and accommodation blocks. The infrastructure was showing its age after 50 years. Sanitation was a problem. Cholera still breaks out here. It was a strange inside-out zoo experience. We were the ones being observed. In the assembly hall we were treated to dance, song, and poetry performances by the inmates.

I sat down with two prisoners, Tina and Phoebe, for one-on-one conversations, with only passive observation from the guards. Tina, aged about 40, told me her story. She had stabbed her husband to death in a drunken rage. She told me how she picked up a knife in the heat of the moment, not knowing what was happening. That moment of choice had led her to where she was now, facing the possibility of a death penalty. Phoebe, aged in her late 20s, had been picked up smuggling drugs into Africa from Hong Kong. She told me her daughter was being looked after by her in-laws, but she couldn't reach her and didn't know what was happening. All because of a choice she made to smuggle drugs. The pain in the eyes of both these women was overwhelming. It was just a moment of choice. I realised the difference between me and the two human beings sitting opposite me was just a thin veil. They were me, if not for the slightest of changes, the tiniest shift of a choice one way or the other.

As I got up to leave, Phoebe asked if she could hug me. The guard nodded. It was a heart-rending connection and one of the deepest, most profound experiences of my life. The idea that it all comes down to choices is so powerful. These two women were no different to any of us. Under different circumstances and had they made different choices, I'm sure they would have gone on to lead normal lives.

I wished they'd had access to system 3 thinking.

EVERYONE HAS STRENGTHS AND WEAKNESSES

Look at your T3 Profile results from chapter 2. In which of the six dimensions did you score medium or high? Give yourself a pat on the back. You have strengths. Remember this as you work on your less developed areas. Everyone has strengths and weaknesses in their system 3 thinking.

In which areas did you score below medium? You will now learn simple (though not always easy) ways to build your strengths in each area. For example, if Focus was a dimension that didn't score high or medium, I will show you how to understand this capability more deeply and give you two practices to build this into a strength. This is one of the most powerful chapters in this book. With the following insights and instructions, you are set to make wiser choices, become more flexible and adaptable, and even enjoy confronting doubt, dilemma, or disruption.

HOW TO ENHANCE FOCUS

When you're faced with a big decision, pay attention to what's going on around you. Focus is a set of skills you can become good at. It means paying sustained attention in the present moment, to notice what is happening. At the same time, focus involves maintaining a still and steady attention on a task. You notice the details. However, when you are deeply focused you also notice the peripheral issues and the impacts they have.

One of the biggest risks in decision-making is being too narrow minded about the problem. If you miss the nuances, you miss the opportunity to see how to craft a more effective decision. With focused attention, you reduce or even eliminate that risk.

Pad man

In November 2016, I interviewed an unassuming inventor from the city of Coimbatore in the South East Indian state of Tamil Nadu. His name was Arunachalam Muruganantham. He had won the Social Enterprise award at the Leadership Energy Summit Asia (LESA) conference in Kuala Lumpur for his work in breaking down the stigma surrounding female menstruation. This is a big issue for impoverished communities globally, where sanitary pads are too expensive for women to afford. He invented a simple machine to produce sanitary pads cheaply.

When I asked Arunachalam about his achievements, he answered with a thick Indian accent. Once he got started, he was hard to stop. As a newlywed in 1998, he spotted his wife carrying something hidden behind her back. He ran behind her and saw a rag cloth, something he wouldn't even use to clean his bicycle. Then he understood she was using this to manage her period days. When he asked her about it, she said she wasn't unaware of menstrual hygiene or sanitary pads, but the expense would eat into the family budget.

He decided to do something to help his wife. He experimented, using his wife as a subject. She wasn't impressed with his early attempts. He asked his sisters. But in a country where menstruation is still largely a taboo subject, they refused to give him feedback. He sought the help of medical college girls, but they refused too. So, he decided to use himself as a test subject. He filled a bottle with animal blood and tied it around his waist with a tube connecting to the sanitary pad he wore. But after two-and-a-half years of research he was nowhere near solving the problem. And, tragically, there was no money left. He faced terrible consequences. His wife divorced him. His mother disowned him. His neighbours were convinced he was perverted.

Arunachalam reached out to various American manufacturers until he found someone willing to explain what made a sanitary pad work. In his small welding workshop, he spent another four years creating his version of the multi-million-dollar machines used to manufacture sanitary pads. By 2006, his machine was being used by many villages in rural India. He won the National Grassroots Technological Innovations Award, and he had a growing reputa-tion as 'India's Menstruation Man'. And then something wonderful happened. His wife read the stories and saw the interviews and returned to be with him after five years apart.

With seed funding, he could make enough sanitary napkin-mak-ing machines to break even. The price tag made it possible for NGOs and self-help women's groups to set up their own sanitary pad manufacturing units in villages. At the time of our interview, hundreds of brands were manufacturing the sanitary pads that he developed, reaching almost every Indian state and close to 20 countries. 'I want to make a low-cost sanitary pad movement across the globe,' he told me. 'I want to make India a 100% sanitary napkin using country, and I want to provide employment to more than a million people in rural India.' Arunachalam had already made it to the TIME 100 Most Influential People List, inspired a documentary, and become a sought-after speaker at the world's best business schools. His life story would later be dramatised in the 2018 Bollywood movie, *Pad Man*.

Arunachalam Muruganantham's story is one of focus. For most men, women's menstruation was a peripheral issue, one that did not concern them. Social stigma further marginalised the issue. But Arunachalam noticed his wife's problem and he focused his attention on how to solve it. He didn't give up. Even when he was rejected by his family and ostracised by his neighbours. He wasn't distracted by it. He continued to focus on the ways and means to provide a low-cost solution, not just for his wife, but for women in rural India and beyond.

The two key practices that will help you enhance focus

Set up a regular practice of mindfulness

According to a survey published by Rasmus Hougaard and Jacqueline Carter in their 2018 book *The Mind of the Leader*, 73% of leaders feel significantly distracted by the demands of other people, competing priorities, general distractions, and excessive workload, And close to 100% of the leaders surveyed said that enhanced focus would be highly valuable.

In a four-month program I conducted for a local health authority in New South Wales in 2013, staff received 10 minutes of daily mindfulness training. This was coupled with one-hour weekly workshops on applying mindfulness at work and developing specific mental strategies. The results were statistically positive. Awareness, focus, and work/life balance improved, while perceived stress reduced. In a shorter four-week program for staff of a health training service in 2014, I also found statistically significant positive effects for awareness, focus, and work/life balance, and reduced perceived stress. And these effects persisted for four weeks after the end of the program.

My research showed that developing the skills of focused attention brings about a calmer, more open and undistracted mind, and greater self-awareness. This improves workplace performance and productivity. For example, one of the participants reported, 'there is definitely a "buzz" around the service regarding mindfulness, and when things happen in meetings, etc., people feel free to remind others to share the "joy" or to take time out to breathe. I believe it has made us more aware of our colleagues and how our behaviour can affect them. It has been a very positive experience and very helpful to the organisation.'

Another participant commented, 'one of the effects of mindfulness training is that it carefully guides my mind to think much more broadly, for the long term and in a way that is sensitive to others – which is a very handy "tool" to have when addressing work-related projects or issues.'

You can train for mindful awareness, and as a consequence develop a capacity for sustained, effortless, and focused attention. Try this daily exercise at home or in your workplace:

1. Set the timer on your phone for 10 minutes.
2. Find a quiet place to sit, and adjust your posture so you are comfortable, with a straight back, and relaxed neck, shoulders,

and arms. Gently close your eyes and allow your breathing to settle into its natural state.

3. For a minute or two, bring your full attention to your breathing. Notice which part of your body is directly connected to your breathing. Perhaps the rise and fall of your abdomen, or the sensation of air moving in and out of your nostrils. Don't try to control it. Let your mind stabilise and settle.

4. Now, let go of your attention to the breath and allow your awareness to open to whatever arises: noises, physical sensations, thoughts, or mental images. Whatever occurs, just be aware of it.

5. Observe without engaging in the experiences. Don't think about it. Don't try to make it go away. Just observe it, neutrally.

6. If you get caught up in the experience of what arises, give the experience a label – for example, *thought, task, calendar* – and then let it go.

7. Whenever you become distracted by thinking about your worries or experiences, remind yourself to *relax, release* from the thought, and *return* your attention to your breath.

8. When the timer sounds, let go of the training and bring your awareness to your present surroundings.

Hit the 'pause button' before making a big decision

As a child in the early 1960s, I remember watching *The Dick Tracy Show* on black-and-white TV. It was a cartoon series in which policeman Dick Tracy fought crime each week, contacting his subordinate flatfoots on his two-way wristwatch radio (presaging the Apple Watch by at least five decades). If one of Tracy's detectives found themselves in sudden danger (bullets speeding towards them, or falling off a cliff) he would yell, 'Hold everything!' The action would obediently screech to a halt and 'wait' while the detective called headquarters for further instructions. Action would resume only after the sign-off catchphrase, 'Six-two and even, over and out' was spoken at the end of the call.

When you're presented with a big decision it may feel as if you're dodging a bullet or falling off a cliff. That's when you need to hold everything, hit the pause button, and step out of the situation, even for a moment.

Igor Grossmann, Associate Professor of Psychology and Director of the Wisdom Research Lab at the University of Waterloo, Ontario, calls this technique 'ego-decentring', which is getting your ego out of the situation and seeing the situation as if you're a fly on the wall. You can look down and see yourself in the situation, struggling with the decision. What would you see from an outside perspective if your ego was not involved?

The dimension of focus is about gaining awareness of all the elements of the situation before making a decision. Hit the pause button and pay attention to what is really happening.

HOW TO ENHANCE LIFE EXPERIENCE

How much life experience do you have? Depending on your age, a lot or not much. Most Asian cultures automatically confer the status of 'wise elder' on their senior citizens. The image of a grey-bearded wizard or a sage in a loin cloth on a mountain top are pervasive archetypes of wisdom. Yet, age is necessary but not sufficient for wisdom according to the Berlin Wisdom Paradigm. You can have very wise Gen Ys and some pretty stupid baby boomers. Length of life is an element of wise decision-making, but it's not the only element.

In a 2005 study, Associate Professor of Sociology at the University of Florida, Monika Ardelt, interviewed a small group of people aged between 59 and 85 years of age. She was looking for distinctions in their experience that matched their responses to her self-administered 'wisdom scale'. She found those who scored high on her scale were able to apply the lessons that life had taught them when they encountered crises and hardship. They learned from their experiences and, as a consequence, recognised and accepted life's unpredictability and uncertainty. Those who scored low demonstrated an avoidance of reflection and an inability or unwillingness to learn from life's lessons. The upshot is that life experience often means doing the same things for longer than anyone else, but not necessarily learning from it.

When people have a debate going on and they don't know what to do, they will turn to the wise person and the wise person will help them make the right choice. People who are wiser are generally the ones more likely to give sage advice. They're drawing down on their own experience and their knowledge of life's trajectory and how people live their lives at different ages and stages.

The idea behind using the dimension of life experience in system 3 thinking is that you are able to draw lessons out of your lived experience and reflect on how to apply those lessons in your own life.

Crossing a few dry gullies

There is an Australian expression which describes someone with experience who may be trusted: 'they've crossed a few dry gullies'. Lieutenant General David Morrison, Chief of the Australian Army, had certainly crossed a few dry gullies in his distinguished military career. I met him in September 2015 soon after his retirement.

He was engaged by Deloitte Australia to present components of our leadership training program for partners. I found him easy to talk to, humble, and surprisingly self-effacing about his career highs and lows. 'When you give the order to send men and women into battle and potentially to their deaths,' he told me, 'they have to look you in the eye and know who you are and what you stand for.' His presentations to the partners were filled with stories about his mistakes and miscalculations as much as his successful campaigns.

David was born into a military family and followed his father, Major General Alan Morrison, into the army in 1979, later graduating from the Officer Cadet School at Portsea and joining the Royal Australian Infantry Corps. By 1991 Morrison had risen to the rank of Major. After graduating from Army Command and Staff College the following year, he was assigned to the brigade that participated in 1994 in Operation Lagoon, a failed attempt to broker a peace agreement between Bougainville secessionists and the government of Papua New Guinea. He was promoted to Colonel in 1999, and to Major General in 2005. He became Deputy Chief of Army in 2008, Forces Commander in 2009, and Lieutenant General in 2011.

Soon after his appointment as Chief of Army in 2011, Morrison had to deal with a series of crises that exposed an underlying culture of sexual degradation and violence, hazing, and abuse within the Army. The ensuing media firestorm prompted an investigation by Sex Discrimination Commissioner Elizabeth Broderick for the Australian Human Rights Commission. She began a dialogue with Morrison about the culture that had allowed such acts to take place. This was a steep learning curve for Morrison, which culminated in a series of audits about how women were treated in the Australian military.

But the culture remained stubbornly resistant. The so-called 'Jedi Council' sex scandal in 2013 triggered his now famous speech on gender equality, with the ultimatum: 'the standard you walk past is the standard you accept'.

Morrison was named Australian of the Year in 2016 for his commitment to gender equality, diversity, and inclusion. Yet he candidly shared with us the lingering acrimony in military circles about his push to eliminate poor attitudes towards women in the Army.

One thing I recall was how he spoke so revealingly about the pain of separation and divorce from his wife and three sons. The honesty with which he reflected on his life and his willingness to impart advice to an audience of senior partners was remarkable. 'Dad, who retired from the Army after almost 30 years of service as a General, was a man of great humility, who understood that difficult decisions have to be made in life,' he said. 'But if they're made for the right ethical reasons, then those difficult decisions need to be stood by. I am incredibly proud to have been his son.'

David Morrison is an exemplar of someone with deep experience of life who has reflected on lessons learned and applied them in organisational leadership and his own personal development.

The two key practices that will help you enhance life experience

Reflect on the lessons of success and failure from your own life

When you're in the pits of despair or things have failed and you've had to crawl your way out, that's a life lesson right there. What did you learn in those moments? And how have you applied that since?

Reflect on these questions:

- What's the most foolish thing I've ever done? What made it foolish?

- What's the wisest thing I've ever done? What made it wise?

In his 2006 book, *Executive Wisdom: Coaching and the emergence of virtuous leaders*, consulting organisational psychologist Richard Kilburg uses similar questions to help leaders explore life lessons of success and failure:

- What is one thing I would most want to change about myself? Why?
- What is one thing I would most like to change in the world? Why?

Reflect on the biographies of others and what it means to live a meaningful life

Every human has a story to tell. And every story has important life lessons. It's better to learn from the failures and successes of others before you make your own mistakes. You can readily access valuable biographies and autobiographies such as:

- *True Compass* by Edward M. Kennedy (2009)
- *Tiger Woods* by Jeff Benedict and Armen Keteyiah (2018)
- *The Program: Seven deadly sins – my pursuit of Lance Armstrong* by David Walsh (2012)
- *I Am Malala: The girl who stood up for education and was shot by the Taliban* by Malala Yousafzai (2014)
- *Elon Musk: How the billionaire CEO of SpaceX and Tesla is shaping our future* by Ashlee Vance (2015)
- *Pour Your Heart Into It: How Starbucks built a company one cup at a time* by Howard Schultz and Dori Jones Yang (1997)
- *Alibaba: The house that Jack Ma built* by Duncan Clark (2016).

The list is endless. Allow yourself to be drawn to the stories of people in history and popular culture you most admire. In this way you can absorb the life lessons of the best and brightest of humanity (and also the crooks, rogues and charlatans).

Some of history's lessons are curated for you, such as:

- *The March of Folly* by Barbara W. Tuchman (1984)
- *This I Believe* by John Marsden (1996)
- *Wisdom* by Andrew Zuckerman (2008).

And of course, there is a torrent of stories, real and fictional, in movies, plays, games, and TV series on streaming platforms. What can you learn from *Game of Thrones*, *Mortal Kombat*, *Schitt's Creek*, *The Good Place*, *The Expanse*, or even *Midsomer Murders*? Popular culture is awash with stories. Which are your favourites? How do they inform your view of the world? What are some important life lessons you've gained from them?

- Name three books, plays, movies, TV series, or other sources of learning which have most instructed you in life lessons?
- What life lessons have you learned?

HOW TO ENHANCE DECISIVENESS

The common, usually mistaken, belief is that you need to sit on top of a mountain and meditate for months or years on end to gain wisdom. But that's not true. To use your wisdom resources to make a difficult decision you need to act in the moment. If you continuously back off and think about it too long, you may let others make the decision. And often the wrong outcomes will happen.

Decisiveness is about being able to choose and not procrastinate. Even *not* making a decision is itself a decision. 'Decisiveness is that you accept uncertainty, you accept diversity of views, and yet you cannot sit on the fence,' says Dr Dilip Jeste from the Stein

Institute for Research in Aging. It's important to consider the available information before making a decision. That needs to happen initially. But there is a moment where you must act, even if you continue debating the decision internally.

Molecules of emotion

At sunset, the Santa Catalina Mountains behind Tucson, Arizona, change from burnt orange to a deep mauve colour. A refreshingly cool desert wind rustles the mesquite trees bordering La Paloma Country Club. It's May 1999 and I'm attending the sixth International Symposium on Functional Medicine. I'm standing at the back of the conference hall on the first day when a middle-aged woman sweeps in. She seems agitated. I offer to help, but she immediately lies down on the floor in a meditative breathing pose. When Dr Candace Pert is announced as the next speaker, my new companion gets up from the floor and makes her way to the stage amid rousing applause from the 400 attendees. That was my introduction to the scientist who narrowly missed out on the Nobel Prize in 1979 for her ground-breaking work on the dynamic information networks linking mind and body. I was a fan. I had brought her book with me from Australia, *Molecules of Emotion: Why you feel the way you feel* (1997), hoping to meet her at the conference. I did. And I still have the book with her signed dedication on the title page.

Candace Pert's journey is a story of decisiveness. In her pharmacology research at Johns Hopkins University in the early 1970s she developed a new methodology to trap the morphine molecule and its receptor in a test tube. This was the end result of multiple trial-and-error decisions. As Pert explains in her book, 'the rule of thumb is to first try the least complex combination of conditions and ingredients, and hope they work.' This leads to a long chain of experiments to find the weakest link. Each decision variable needs to be tried and tested. While working at the National Institute of Mental Health from 1975 to 1987 she published over two hundred scientific papers. Pert was always driven by her faith in science as a search for the truth. Experimental discoveries are sometimes the result of accidents, but they always emerge through repeated decisions.

Her work with immunologist Michael Ruff was instrumental in the development of the new field of psychoneuroimmunology (PNI) in the mid 1980s. 'The neuropeptides and their receptors probably represent the biochemical substrate of emotion,' Pert wrote. 'The molecules of emotion.'

Decisiveness can take strange, even counterintuitive turns. I attended Candace Pert and Michael Ruff's workshop at the The Psychology of Health, Immunity and Disease Conference at Hilton Head Island, South Carolina. It was a cold and windswept December in 2000 when I took up my seat in the front row of the room, notebook in hand. I was excited to learn about the complex dynamics of PNI from the scientists who virtually invented the field. But Candace and Michael got us up out of our chairs and workshopped various methods of sensing each other through holding hands and chanting. I was dumbfounded. I came for the biochemistry, but I got mysticism. During the break, I asked them where was the evidence for their strange new approach? 'We know the body and mind are one,' said Candace. 'So, we made the decision to explore the deeper connections.' Michael added, 'We know the science will catch up, but we don't want to wait.'

And that's what the dimension of decisiveness means. Not waiting for permission or for all the information to be available but taking action anyway.

The two key practices that will help you enhance decisiveness

Increase the frequency of your day-to-day decision-making

Get used to making smaller decisions because they add up to larger ones. For example, you're going out to lunch with friends and somebody says let's go to that great restaurant down the road. Okay, great. Let's do that. What should we have? Oh, why don't we all have the laksa? Okay, sure, sounds all right to me.

But you're letting other people make decisions for you. Sometimes it's easier to do that. But what happens if you start making decisions and get used to making decisions? No, I don't want to go to that restaurant. No, I want to have mushroom risotto.

The idea is to get practised and comfortable making small decisions. Developing this capability will increase the likelihood that you'll make a wise choice when you're faced with a moment of doubt, dilemma, or disruption in the future.

You could also seek permission from your friends or colleagues: 'I'm practising decisiveness, I'm probably going to make decisions that may or may not go over very well but please give me the opportunity to become more decisive.' That way, you won't rub people up the wrong way unnecessarily.

Make smaller decisions building up to a big one: fail fast, frequently, and frugally

The American inventor, Thomas Edison (1847–1931), famously defined genius as, '1% inspiration; 99% perspiration'. His method was to test an idea to see if it works, reject or refine it, and try again; making small decisions, which most often lead to failure. Linda Hall, Greg Brandeau, Emily Truelove, and Kent Lineback, authors of the 2014 book *Collective Genius: The art and practice of leading innovation*, say innovation requires a mindset of try, learn, adjust, try again. They studied leaders of innovative companies such as Pixar Animation Studios, Google, eBay, HCL Technologies, Pfizer, and IBM to uncover the 'magic sauce' of innovation. Despite differences in culture, age, and gender, the leaders they studied had some common personal characteristics. Chief among these was being 'holistic thinkers, yet action oriented'. These leaders were ready to try new things, to experiment over and over. They knew that solutions emerged from trial and error, which made them decisive in taking action.

Pip Marlow, the former CEO of Microsoft Australia and later CEO of Salesforce ANZ, said in an interview in January 2020, 'You have to create a safe space to trial things and potentially fail.' Marlow expressed the need to invest in the capabilities and culture to support innovation, which is 'to support failing fast, frequently and frugally, so to speak'.

Make many smaller decisions to build to a big decision, recognising that the risk of failure may be lower than the risk of *not* making the decision. This is the dimension of decisiveness.

HOW TO ENHANCE COMPASSION

Compassion is central to the idea of wise decision-making. Compassion literally means 'to suffer together'. From the experience of shared suffering comes the motivation to help relieve the suffering of others. His Holiness the Dalai Lama positions this beautifully when he comments on the decisions made by world leaders. 'It's all about compassion and recognising the common good,' he says. 'We're all on this planet together and every decision affects every single one of us.'

How can you make decisions that consider the effects on other people? You need to be more sensitive to the needs and wants of others and be able to respond to those needs. For example, Bill and Melinda Gates, through the Bill and Melinda Gates Foundation, have donated the majority of their vast wealth to make a difference in underdeveloped countries. They are focused on improving people's health and giving them the chance to lift themselves out of hunger and extreme poverty. The contribution they're making is a deeply compassionate one. They want to be able to turn over their immense resources to the common good of humanity. That's what is meant by compassion.

You may not feel compassionate when compared to the Dalai Lama or Bill and Melinda Gates. But don't beat yourself up. You are hard-wired for compassion. Start with self-compassion. If you're compassionate with yourself, you're more likely to be compassionate with others. Compassion training, or *Tonglen* in the Buddhist tradition, starts with wishing for good things for yourself, then wishing for good things for the people you know, and finally wishing for good things for the people you don't know.

What's the difference between sympathy, empathy, kindness, and compassion? Sympathy is feeling pity or sorrow for someone else's suffering. Empathy is imagining what it must be like to experience that suffering – putting yourself in their shoes. Kindness is the quality of being friendly, generous, and considerate towards someone who is suffering. Compassion on the other hand is the quality of being merciful and taking action to alleviate another's suffering. The component of action is what separates compassion from empathy, sympathy, or kindness. It is the knowledge that there can never really be any peace and joy for me until there is peace and joy finally for you.

Under the Bodhi tree

It is 14 February 2012 at 11 am. We are sitting under the most famous Bodhi tree in the world at the Mahabodhi Temple in Bodhgaya, North East India. It is a hot and dusty Indian morning. American scientist and Buddhist monk Alan Wallace, principal of the Santa Barbara Institute for Consciousness Studies, is teaching at the very place where the Buddha gained enlightenment 2,500 years ago. All around us are groups of chanting, praying, prostrating devotees from all corners of the planet. As a rational science-trained psychologist I have been pursuing the Buddhist 'science of mind'. But now Alan has reduced the combined efforts of psychology, sociology, philosophy and neuroscience to just the last of seven points the Buddha made about consciousness. 'Neuroscience can only substantiate the neural correlates of mental cognition but has nothing to say about where consciousness comes from,' he says. 'Just as Galileo saw the phases of Venus with direct observation through a refined instrument, so the Buddha used his refined mind as an instrument to observe the nature of consciousness.' Science rejects first-person observation as unverifiable. But, Alan points out that focused attention is a way to develop our own instrument to observe the mind. Consistent, empirical evidence from first-person observations has been collected and collated in thousands of texts over hundreds of years. It turns out Western science is late to the party. Alan tells us compassion is key to understanding the Buddha's teachings. Compassion is our most powerful, most ubiquitous response. 'Imagine a mother's love,' Alan says. 'Now imagine that love for every sentient being to get a sense of the scope and depth of the Buddha's compassion.'

Derived from the Buddha's wisdom, system 3 thinking encompasses focus and compassion, two essential elements of mind.

The two key practices that will help you enhance compassion

Practise random acts of kindness – giving without expecting recognition or reward

Kindness is compassion on training wheels. If you can be kind to yourself and others, and if you can practise that kindness, then it extends out, because kindness is generally something you do for another person. It's a very direct and deliberate action and has an immediate response. You're being kind if you're allowing somebody to go ahead of you in the shopping queue. Or you're being kind if you're helping an elderly person cross the street.

Compassion is a broader, more global version of kindness. Compassion is opening up to that one act of kindness and how that plays out across not just your community but across the state, across the nation, and globally. How can you express that kindness in a much broader, more universal way? Kindness is a state of mind and also a component of compassion.

Start with random acts of kindness. It's a bit like decisiveness. If you can start making small decisions, it will build up to you being able to make big decisions when the time comes. So, if you can start with small random acts of kindness, it's likely to build up to compassion when the time comes. You have to be compassionate with yourself as well as with others.

For example, a number of cafes have the idea of paying it forward. You pay for your coffee plus an extra one, and that way if someone really needs it but can't afford it or has left their wallet at home, they can benefit from that act of kindness. You're not doing it for the thanks or for the reward to your ego. You're doing it because it's coming from a deeper place.

Or you might volunteer to work in a migrant centre or to distribute surplus food to homeless communities. There are abundant opportunities to demonstrate kindness and acts of compassion, through deliberate action and dedication of your time.

Kindness is a proxy for compassion. You can practise that first and it opens you up to the notion of compassion.

Pay attention to injustice, ignorance, cruelty, and selfishness in the world

The leadership programs that I and my colleagues at ICLIF (International Centre for Leadership in Finance) conducted in Asia would include what we called an 'immersion experience'. If we were in Bangkok running a six-day leadership program, we would take participants to a school for homeless children in the slums. In Ho Chi Minh City we would bring participants to a mission caring for elderly and infirm adults who have no family and no one to visit them. We'd listen to the staff tell their stories. Then we would engage in an act of service; for example, participating with the children at playtime, or preparing meals and feeding the residents.

One of the immersion experiences I helped organise was with BJCK (Buku Jalanan Chow Kit, which means 'school on the street') in the seedy Chow Kit area of central Kuala Lumpur. Co-founder Siti Rahayu Baharain started the program in an alleyway with classes twice a week. The children would sit on mats placed on the ground, diligently listening to the tutors – mostly students from neighbouring universities – and scribbling in their books lit up by flashlights and solar lamps. Thanks to corporate and community sponsorship, BJCK moved to a safe indoor venue in late 2017. Many of the children have immigrant parents with no papers so they are effectively stateless. Through no fault of their own they are denied access to Malaysian society. Their only hope is to pass a final exam at the end of their schooling, through which they may be granted residency and access to university.

Many of these students have been successful. Siti Rahayu has a bubbly and optimistic personality and a deep passion for education as a pathway out of poverty and disadvantage. 'We seek to inspire the children and provide them with hope and opportunities,' she says. 'Everything here is based on trust and love.' I worked closely with her to include BJCK children and teachers in some of our leadership programs. Participants were often so moved by Siti Rahayu's example of compassion that they took up sponsorship of teachers and resources for the school out of their own pockets.

HOW TO ENHANCE EMOTIONAL REGULATION

Harvard Medical School psychologist Dr Susan David is the best-selling author of *Emotional Agility* (2016). She talks about how emotional regulation is recognising what your hot buttons are and noticing what gets you riled up, then gently sidestepping your buttons and not letting your emotions rule your decisions. Being able to identify what you're feeling as something that's separate to you is an emotional intelligence competency. It's creating space between the feeling and the way you're thinking about that feeling. For example, you're in traffic and someone cuts you off. You can be really angry at that moment. But emotion regulation is identifying that you're actually frustrated about that person cutting in. Why is that person cutting in? There may be a reason why they're doing that. Rather than blast your horn at them, you might offer the wish for them to get to where they're going (but perhaps not as quickly as they might want).

Emotional regulation is about keeping your cool but also not simmering or suppressing your emotions. You're saying, 'I can see that I'm angry about this situation. But if I put that anger to one side for the moment and just really sit and listen to what's happening, I'll learn much more about what's going on, and therefore, I'm more likely to choose wisely.'

The emotionally intelligent CEO

In the afternoon of 27 April 1977, we were all called to an impromptu townhall meeting in the Perth offices of Agnew Mining Company. I was the Personnel Research Officer, hired five months earlier by the CEO, Barry. He had discovered the new field of Organisation Development during a course at Harvard Business School the previous year, and he wanted an 'OD practitioner' to advise on the design and operation of the company and the new township of Leinster at the mine site over 300 kilometres north of Kalgoorlie in the Great Victoria Desert.

At the time, most of us occupied a single floor of the National Australia Bank building on St Georges Terrace. Only a few were at the mine site during the construction phase. It didn't take long for us to gather in the boardroom.

Barry was ashen-faced.

He told the room that five miners had been killed in an accident at the mine site that morning. Apparently, the winder in the headframe over the mineshaft had malfunctioned. Instead of lowering the bucket carrying the men down into the mineshaft it had inexplicably reversed. The bucket accelerated up and collided with the headframe, flinging the occupants into the air.

This was the first multiple fatality of any mining operation in Western Australia since 1951. The company mining engineer on site was my age and, like me, he had only graduated the year before. We were all shocked.

Barry's only concern was for those miners and their families, not his company. That afternoon was the first and only time I have ever seen a CEO weep openly. His compassion was on display and we were all moved by it. There were more than a few tears in the room. Barry displayed an authenticity in his grief that day that became the hallmark for me of what it means to be an emotionally intelligent CEO. He could have chosen to hide his feelings from us that day, but he didn't.

The two key practices that will help you enhance emotional regulation

Identify and name what you're feeling as emotions arise

You can be overly optimistic or overly pessimistic. Those emotions have the potential to lead you astray. Even when you're feeling happy, you don't always make the right decision. In choosing wisely, you need to be cool about your emotions but not ignore them. Wise decisions do utilise emotions. For example, a deep feeling of sadness could be a strong prompt to make a wiser choice.

Richard Rohr, American Franciscan priest and founder of the Center for Action and Contemplation in Albuquerque, New Mexico, talks about how, in our happy, positive society, we tend to ignore or try to stifle grief and pain. But in sitting with pain and grief, there is wisdom because those sorts of emotions can actually be teachers.

Your feelings *are* relevant at the moment of choice. The key to making a wise choice is to leverage the emotion, rather than letting the emotion lead the way.

Don't take things personally: acknowledge others' emotional responses without taking responsibility for them

'Don't Take Anything Personally' is the second of four agreements you can make with yourself to break free of society's rules of 'domestication', according to Mexican author and spiritualist Don Miguel Ruiz. He was born in rural Mexico, attended medical school, and became a neurosurgeon in Tijuana. But a near-fatal car accident changed the course of his life. He left medicine to examine the essential truth about life and humanity through his mother's ancestral knowledge of ancient Toltec traditions. He apprenticed himself to a shaman, and eventually moved to the United States.

Taking things personally is the maximum expression of selfishness, Ruiz says. It's the assumption that everything is about 'me'. When you take responsibility for how others are feeling you set yourself up for suffering. Others will blame you for 'making' them feel a particular way. You will be forever the cause of their suffering and they will want you to 'pay' for it. 'You are never responsible for the actions of others; you are only responsible for you. When you truly understand this, and refuse to take things personally, you can hardly be hurt by the careless comments or actions of others', says Ruiz.

When you see yourself as the agent of your own life, you are at the centre of your feelings and your destiny. From that position, it's much easier to identify your emotions and control them rather than have them control you. However, thinking about your emotions is difficult. They seem to arise spontaneously. 'The devil made me do it!' It's a tough ask to try to separate yourself from those feelings. When you realise that you are at the centre of the choices you make, it's possible to observe your emotions rather than be subjected to them.

HOW TO ENHANCE TOLERANCE FOR DIVERGENT VALUES

You have a set of values which you live your life by, but other people have different values. Can you acknowledge that? How do you accept others' values without denying your own values?

In my experiences of working and travelling throughout Asia, I came across lots of different value systems, particularly when training leaders from different countries and different cultures. There are racial and religious overtones that are quite self-evident and seen as more acceptable in many Asian societies than in Western societies. The first time I greeted a Muslim woman in Malaysia, I naturally extended my hand but she recoiled. It was a shock to me. But then I realised the cultural sensitivity around women touching a man's hand. From then on, I consciously made a note and embraced their cultural method of greeting: placing the right hand over one's heart. Quite charming really.

Tolerance is about seeing these differences in context and understanding the historical precedent behind them. For example, in Malaysia there have been successive waves of Portuguese, Dutch, and British colonialist incursions. They've also had the Japanese and the Chinese come in, take the wealth from the country and leave. Trying to protect the citizens from these sorts of racial situations is something that has become ingrained.

It's also about relative values. We all think we're honest until somebody asks, 'Do I look fat in this?' How well did you score on Tolerance for Divergent Values in the T3 Profile? If you scored in the high range, this suggests that you've got a broad acceptance of the variations of beliefs, spiritual practices and values across human communities. It also suggests you're not easily offended. But if you scored low on Tolerance for Divergent Values, it suggests that while you may recognise differences in beliefs, spiritual practices, and values, you firmly adhere to your own value system. However, that view doesn't allow for the flexibility to see what another person might be perceiving in a situation and what might be the moral value of what they're seeing, compared to what you're seeing.

A river in Egypt

In December 2017 I was in Khartoum, the capital of Sudan. My colleagues and I from ICLIF (International Centre for Leadership In Finance) had been invited by the Central Bank of Sudan to present executive education for the bank's associate and senior directors.

My part of the program was on leadership in the 21st century and coaching for wise decision-making. I had a dozen participants crowded into a small training room on the fourth floor of the impressive Central Bank of Sudan office tower. A colleague had shown me how to write my name in Arabic, which I did on the flip chart to open the program. I was off to a great start. But when I got to the research and practice of how to make wise decisions, the group was vociferous. 'We expect the Qur'an to teach us what wisdom is,' they said. 'We know how to make wise decisions according to our faith. We don't need any of this!' I explained how wisdom has deep spiritual significance for all faiths. But there are times when your religion, although necessary, is not sufficient for helping you to solve the complex problems of the 21st century. 'I am offering a third system of thinking to help you make wise decisions,' I said. 'Denial isn't a positive strategy for a central bank facing international sanctions.' And then, as I had said in many of my workshops back in Australia, 'and denial isn't a river in Egypt.'

The room fell silent.

In that moment, I realised two things: Sudan's historical enemy is Egypt. And 'de' Nile was visible from the training room window. I had failed to appreciate the diversity of values in the room. Worse, I had demonstrated an intolerance to values which were significantly different to my own.

The two key practices that will help you enhance tolerance for divergent values

Practise curiosity about other cultures, beliefs, and values

You're not giving up your own values by acknowledging that others may hold different values to yours. You're using their values in an informing role. Participants of some of the leadership programs I conducted in Malaysia would openly declare their entitlement to government services and special consideration because 'we are Bumiputra' (literally, 'people of the soil'). They believed it was right that they should be looked after ahead of other races. And yet, in workshop exercises where we instructed groups to come up with their vision for the future of Malaysia, there was a lot more inclusiveness, recognition of diversity, and an acknowledgement of the strengths of society because of that diversity. That was a way of acknowledging the racial differences present in the room.

It was deeply distressing for me, living in a Muslim country and seeing the way Australian right-wing political actors like Pauline Hanson were reported in the Malaysian media. The reality of living in another country is acknowledging the local cultural values without taking offence or believing that they somehow impinge on your own value system.

*Notice what triggers a judgmental response in you and
seek to be more flexible*

One of the experimental conditions from the Berlin Wisdom
Paradigm was to instruct the experimental subject to 'imagine that
you're on a magic carpet and you're flying around the world, looking down on different cultures and different cities and towns'. This
had the effect of enhancing the quality of their decision making.
Why? Because acknowledging the diversity of values in the world
triggered them to widen their perspective.

Check on how inconsistent you are with your own values. Test
yourself. The next time your child comes home with a really awful
painting from school, do you say, 'Darling, that's horrible, I hate it'?
Or do you say, 'That's wonderful, you're so creative and expressive'.
We can be very inconsistent in applying our values.

It's easy to make a mistake and assume your own value system
holds sway when there is another culture, set of beliefs, or historical precedent in play. But if you take that into account, you can
make better decisions.

Compassionate bankers

It's a cool, tropical sunrise on the Malaysian island of Langkawi.
Early morning rain clouds, tinged with pink, have been chased out
across the Andaman Sea. It's the last day of a four-day residential
leadership program for Associate Directors of the Central Bank of
Malaysia, during which they were introduced to system 3 thinking.
It is early October 2017, and the historic change of government
won't occur until the following year. But nobody knows that yet.
The 20 participants are a sample of the country's best and brightest,
but they have been struggling with the dictatorial demands of their
new governor. I am the lead faculty, co-designer and co-facilitator

of the program along with my colleagues from ICLIF (International Centre for Leadership In Finance). In designing this program, we received instruction from the governor to make sure it connected the participants with their core duty to the nation.

Now, as the sea breeze stirs the palms along Cenang beach, I reflect on how the program achieved these objectives. Participants were encouraged to think differently using system 3 thinking. We incorporated a daily practice of mindful focus. Participants completed the 'life-line' exercise to reflect on lessons from their life experience to date. We set up a 'truth circle' with a visiting executive director who listened to the hurt and frustration being experienced by the participants. Then we taught emotional intelligence skills to help them better regulate their own and others' emotions.

One day we collaborated with a local bicycle shop to deliver boxes of unassembled children's bicycles. Three teams received one box each. They had to assemble their bicycle and prove it was safe to ride within the allocated time. There were no assembly instructions, but each team was given three questions they could ask the bicycle shop proprietor. This was an exercise in decisiveness. At the end, teams were rank ordered by speed, process, and safety.

After lunch the following day, we introduced the group to the founder of the Langkawi Charity Club. She told us about the hidden poverty on Langkawi, despite the island being an international tourist destination. She explained how their charity struggled to support families in need. We had pre-ordered food and household items and the three teams were instructed to make up care packages. This challenged some participants to set aside their own values and tolerate the reality of others' lives. Teams were then assigned to a bus which would take them to meet with a family selected by the charity club. Just before departure, the bicycle each team had assembled the previous day was loaded onto the bus. On arrival, teams distributed their care package, including the assembled children's bicycle which had been allocated for a child in each family.

The young girl in the family my team and I visited didn't know how to ride. One of the participants spent time teaching her so that she was confident by the time we left. The experience of seeing such stark poverty face to face in an abundant country like Malaysia was confronting for many of the participants. Yet, it was a reminder that over the future course of their careers, they would be required to make compassionate decisions on behalf of the national interest.

TWELVE WAYS TO ENHANCE YOUR SYSTEM 3 THINKING

I've derived these techniques for enhancing your system 3 thinking from my experience in executive coaching, psychological therapy, and conducting executive education programs over a number of years. This is how you can practically become a wiser decision maker.

The practice of enhancing your system 3 thinking

If **focus** was a dimension for which you did not score in the high range, practising mindfulness is a very good thing to do. Most senior leaders I've met include mindfulness practice as a key part of their daily schedule. Mindfulness has its origins in the Buddhist practice of understanding your moment-to-moment experience, to gradually develop self-knowledge and wisdom. Buddhist teachings describe wisdom as seeing things just as they are – a requisite for the complete freedom from suffering.

If **life experience** was a dimension where you think you could have scored higher, take time to reflect on lessons from your own life. Sometimes getting a good mentor or a coach to help you ask the right questions and reflect on those lessons can be quite powerful and effective.

If **decisiveness** was not in the high range for you, just start making decisions. Lots of small decisions. Don't wait until you have to make a big decision. Get used to making little decisions. Make a game of it. For example, decide what you're going to eat from the menu before anybody else does. Choose a television show to watch without flicking through the options for 30 minutes.

For **compassion**, reflect on actions of kindness and fairness and justice. Notice current affairs where injustice is happening. Pay attention to those events. Think about what you might do in that situation. What might be a better response? How could you practise compassion under those circumstances?

For **emotional regulation**, realise that you actually have a rich and balanced emotional life. Draw on that emotional life. Learn to identify the emotions you're feeling. Learn to see your emotions as a reservoir you can draw on to help you make good decisions.

For **tolerance for divergent values**, be curious about other beliefs and values. Become aware of the vast tapestry of value systems, beliefs, and principles of action throughout human societies. See what other people believe and what they value.

Remember the 12 techniques to make wiser choices when you're faced with doubt, dilemma, or disruption:

Focus:
- Set up a regular practice of mindfulness: 10 minutes per day observing your breathing.
- Hit the 'pause button' before making a big decision.

Life experience:
- Reflect on the lessons of success and failure from your own life.
- Reflect on the biographies of others and what it means to live a meaningful life.

Decisiveness:
- Increase the frequency of your day-to-day decision-making.
- Make smaller decisions building up to a big one: fail fast, frequently, and frugally.

Compassion:
- Practise random acts of kindness – giving without expecting recognition or reward.
- Pay attention to injustice, ignorance, cruelty, and selfishness in the world.

Emotional regulation:
- Identify and name what you're feeling as emotions arise.
- Don't take things personally: acknowledge others' emotional responses without taking responsibility for them.

Tolerance for divergent values:
- Practise curiosity about other cultures, beliefs and values.
- Notice what triggers a judgmental response in you and seek to be more flexible.

CONCLUSION

System 3 thinking is a skill, and – like any skill – you can learn it. It is made up of six dimensions which act like capabilities. You can improve these capabilities, so don't lose heart if you're medium or low in any of these areas. I've given you some suggestions about how to increase or improve each of the six dimensions.

Take the time to practise. Because there is going to come a decision moment in your life when you will need system 3 thinking. I've already shared a few of mine. No one I've worked with has ever scored low on all six dimensions – so, you should have a few dimensions to work with. Start with whichever dimension feels most appropriate or most comfortable. If you feel stuck, start with the one you scored lowest on or the one that was the most surprising to you.

WHAT'S COMING UP NEXT?

We'll look at examples of when choices go bad and how system 3 thinking might have helped. It's a good idea to learn from other people's mistakes before you make your own. By the time you're trying to figure out whether to cross a bridge in your life or not it may be too late to start learning the skills of system 3 thinking. Better to practise now so you can choose wisely when the time comes.

When choices go bad

Many decisions have unintended consequences. What seemed like a good idea at the time can turn out to be disastrous over the long term. Ethical considerations are necessary but not sufficient. What's needed is a deep practice of wisdom which can be applied at the moment of choice.

Last call

Flight AN151 climbed out over the city lights of Brisbane en route to Sydney on a cloudy evening. Curiously I noticed the faint sound of a mobile phone ringing above the rushing noise of the engines. The ringing sound was getting closer. And then I saw the phone gliding down the inclined aisle from where it had been dropped up ahead, past where I was sitting and on towards the back of the plane, much to the amusement of my fellow passengers. 'ET phone home!' someone called out. 'Long distance!' someone else said. 'Last call!' The cabin went quiet. That last comment was bitter-sweet. It was Tuesday 11 September, 2001. Everyone knew that Australia's legacy carrier for 65 years, Ansett Airlines, was on the verge of collapse and we were on one of the last flights. What we didn't know was what was about to happen in New York City overnight, Australian time.

Ansett Airlines was officially grounded on Friday 24 September, 2001. It was the biggest corporate shutdown and layoff in Australia's history with 16,500 staff losing their jobs. My brother, who was an Ansett B767 First Officer at the time, was one of them. What began as a series of business choices over 20 years ended up being a very bad choice for the professional, passionate, and loyal Ansett workforce and their families who had to fight for fair compensation for more than a decade.

Transport magnate, the late Sir Peter Abeles, was chairman of Ansett Airlines in the 1980s. He was passionate about turning Ansett into the world's best domestic airline. Instead of a stream-lined operation he ordered a disparate aircraft fleet and he installed a luxurious first class for the first time in Australian domestic avi-ation. His 50% business partner was Rupert Murdoch, who gave Abeles free rein with Ansett as he concentrated on building his media empire in the US and UK, using Ansett as a cash cow. This put Ansett on the back foot when deregulation started in 1990. Amidst the jostling for air rights, Air New Zealand acquired 50% of Ansett Holdings Limited in 1996 giving it a stake in the Australian domestic market. But cultural differences made for a rocky mar-riage and potential cost savings were lost. When Singapore Airlines made a play for Rupert Murdoch's 50% share of Ansett in late 1999 Air New Zealand blocked the sale and bought out the rest of Ansett, paying top dollar. Singapore Airlines was forced to become a minority shareholder. Consequent management upheavals in

Ansett and Air New Zealand happened just as Richard Branson's Virgin Blue and Impulse Airlines started flying with a cost structure half that of Ansett's. In early 2000, Air New Zealand was forced to concede to the Australian Stock Exchange that Ansett was losing money. A new CEO, former Qantas deputy CEO Gary Toomey, was appointed to run the combined Air New Zealand–Ansett group. Despite making good choices, in early 2001 Toomey became the lightning rod for the eventual collapse of the airline. Ansett was losing $18 million per week. Backroom negotiation was going on between Singapore Airlines, Qantas, Richard Branson, and the New Zealand government. For staff in both airlines it was 'gut wrenching'. Everyone wanted to believe there was hope. But when the receivers took over in September 2001 it was clear the demise of Ansett was due to a series of choices that had gone bad.

APPLYING SYSTEM 3 THINKING

In this chapter I'll show you how to use everything you've found out about your own decision-making over the previous chapters. We'll start with some stories of choices going bad – sometimes disastrously so. Then I'll also explain how to make better decisions in the fields of business and in government and in your own life.

I want to demonstrate how the process of choosing wisely is a practical one and how it can be used pragmatically. You may think that being wise and wisdom itself is something that's beyond reach – that you should be sitting in a loincloth on top of a mountain – but that's not true. You already have the resources to make wise choices.

Remember, system 3 thinking is a balance between system 1 and system 2 thinking. You only utilise system 3 thinking when you're faced with a situation where there is no right or wrong answer, where you have no a roadmap of how to proceed, or you don't know what the outcome is going to be. In a way, system 3 thinking is used more rarely in terms of day-to-day problems .

It's certainly possible to make serious mistakes in your life. Many people say, 'I live with no regrets'. But the reality is that everyone's story is unique. It's important as you get older to utilise system 3 thinking more fully. In the early stages of your life cycle, you're pretty much reliant on system 1 thinking. It's all about me, me, me and want, want, want. Then, when you make mistakes, you draw on system 2 thinking to rationalise your behaviour. But as you get older, you realise that it's not just about you and it's not just about your family either. It's about the wider community and what you can do to give back. System 3 thinking emerges naturally if you mature through the normal lifecycle. That's why wisdom is more often found in older people. They've had more time to make mistakes and reflect on that. And they've had more time to think about how to balance system 1 and system 2 thinking.

Developing the skills of system 3 thinking enables you to have better mental fitness in dealing with the circumstances of your life. If you let go of the need for self-satisfaction represented by system 1 thinking and you let go of the self-justification represented by system 2 thinking, then system 3 thinking opens up a field of possibilities and opportunities. It's not the same as magical thinking, which sounds like, 'if I think positively, it will happen'. But if you change your mental attitude it changes the way you approach your circumstances. This is where system 3 thinking can be a great gift in later life and for anyone facing trying circumstances at any stage of life.

WHEN THINGS GO BAD

One of the problems that occurs persistently in big decisions made by governments and business and in life is that decision makers fail to step back and think about the process of the decision. They tend to think about the outcomes, and then jump either forward or backwards from that position. Unless you step back and think not just about the decision but the way in which the decision is being made, you're liable to make foolish decisions.

Consensus is thought to be the best possible outcome for a decision. But consensus only comes about when there is already a lot that's known about the decision. This leads to various techniques and strategies to negotiate a consensus outcome. In many instances, however, decision makers don't have all the information, or can't even predict what the outcome might be. Sometimes achieving consensus is the worst thing to do. It narrows the views of all concerned and leads to a less effective decision.

Let's look at some examples of when choices go bad and see how system 3 thinking might have prevented disastrous outcomes.

When the world economy almost collapsed

The financial crisis of 2008–10, however you define it historically (the Atlantic crisis, the Global Financial Crisis) showed that choices made by individual actors in banks, mortgage broking firms, and government regulatory agencies could definitely go bad.

What seemed like a good idea at the time – packaging up mortgage risk and on-selling to 'subprime' mortgages to get more people into their own homes – quickly unravelled when enough people couldn't afford the payments and simply handed back the keys. Then, with the resulting failure of Lehman Brothers and other financial institutions, the world suffered a near complete collapse of the financial system.

A group of researchers from the Department of Experimental Psychology and Cognitive Science at Justus Liebig University, Giessen, Germany, undertook a business simulation in 2010 to find out what might have happened. They ran a simulation of all the stock prices leading up to and during the financial crisis. They allocated two groups of subjects who had to make individual decisions about what to buy and what to sell. One group of subjects were experienced stockbrokers. The other group were meteorologists. The degree of error of their decisions could be tracked. That is, was it a good decision to buy? Or should they have sold?

What they found was that the experienced stockbrokers made many more invalid and implausible errors than the meteorologists. They also made more valid and implausible errors than the meteorologists. In fact, the meteorologists would have done better if they'd been running Lehman Brothers! Okay, that may be an exaggeration, but why were the experienced stockbrokers so bad in the simulation compared to others who had no experience in financial markets? The reason – the researchers concluded – was belief bias.

If new information doesn't support your existing belief about something, you'll rationalise anything to confirm your belief. You believe it to be true and so you'll justify it. This is what happened with the stockbrokers in the experiment. They basically rode the market down the way the real stockbrokers in the financial crisis did. They weren't as *decisive* as they made out. The researchers weren't saying that this is what caused the financial collapse. What they were saying was it's interesting to see how bias probably played a part, and probably a much more significant part than we'll ever know.

The financial actors in the crisis almost certainly expected the future to play out in the same way as the past. Short-term gain has a habit of blinding people to long-term pain. Did anyone contemplate the essence (or common sense) of what was happening? Clearly, no one asked themselves the moral question, 'what might other people think or feel who are watching me make this decision?' Had they stepped back and sensed the emerging future being created through their actions they might have changed course.

The crisis might have been averted in the first place if system 3 thinking was more widely distributed. Senior financial actors had access to *life experience*. They had seen these sorts of things happen before. Yet, many of them still tried to game the system. The 2010 German study which simulated the trading conditions of the time confirmed that experience is often just doing the same thing over and over.

There was probably a lack of *focus* on the real market indicators at the time. Perhaps financial actors were only looking for the upside and ignoring the potential for loss. Certainly, there was a lot of emotional expression in the executive committees and boardrooms of financial institutions and government agencies as the crisis unfolded according to observers. Could they have made better decisions if they accessed the skills of *emotional regulation*? Lack of sufficient *diversity* of thinking by decision making groups might also have contributed. When everyone looks the same, sounds the same, and comes from the same Ivy League business schools, there's a higher likelihood of groupthink – a psychological condition in which the desire for group cohesion overpowers the individual who criticises the group decision, even when that individual is right. By far the most significant dimension of system 3 thinking missed during the crisis was *compassion*. Pitifully little attention was given to the potential suffering of shareholders, investors, mortgagees, and their families. Or to the suffering of businesses and the erosion of capital value, leading to great financial and psychological distress. The choices of a relatively few financial actors had a ripple effect that ended up destroying the lives and the livelihoods of millions of people all over the world.

The Sydney light rail gets heavy

In 2012, the New South Wales state government rushed to get the Sydney Light Rail project signed off before the state election in an effort to secure another term for the Premier, Gladys Berejiklian. The Sydney Light Rail project was designed to carry people through George Street, the main thoroughfare of Sydney, right out to the universities and hospitals of the eastern suburbs. The construction would mean closing down the major business precinct in Sydney for a period of time.

What came to light was that the state government had withheld information to get this signed off quickly. They didn't reveal that the excavation work along the path of the light rail was going to turn up a lot of relics, Aboriginal sites, underground water pipes, and underground wiring. All of these things were not featured in the plan. The construction company kept adding on costs for this. Every time they'd dig, they'd find a piece of wiring or a piece of pipe, or an Aboriginal relic.

It was causing enormous delays to the project. The State Government baulked at paying out more money. They came to an impasse. In the end, the State Government had to cough up an enormous amount of money to get the project completed. Finally, it was opened in late 2019 at a cost of over $3.1bn, from an initial budget of $1.6bn in 2012.

There are lots of factors involved in making such decisions. Anyone involved in a big project realises there are lots of moving parts, including external circumstances that the project manager might not have any control over. But where there is a measure of doubt, where there are dilemmas to be solved, or where there's significant disruption, it's helpful to stop and contemplate the process of decision-making.

Paul C. Nutt is a Professor of Management Sciences and Public Policy and Management in the Fisher College of Business at Ohio State University. He researched big project decision failures over a 20-year period. The Sydney light rail debacle is a classic case of what Nutt calls an 'idea imposition process' of decision-making.

The idea imposed by the NSW Premier was evaluated on its engineering merits and contracts were awarded relatively quickly. *Emotional regulation* was suspended in the political heat of an election campaign. The Premier would have been insistent: 'just get it signed because I want to get re-elected.'

Focus wasn't given to the community benefits but rather to a single idea driven by the Premier, 'We need to do this. We can't delay. We have to get it done.' A cost-benefit analysis wasn't commissioned before the start of the project, so the likely social and economic knock-on effects were never questioned. The project could have benefitted from harnessing a *diversity* of views and values. When the cost benefit analysis was eventually done it showed an unfavourable balance. So, a new appraisal was prepared for the NSW government in 2013. This shifted the cost-benefit ratio to positive after incorporating 'non-conventional' economic benefits, through monetising the value ascribed to a project by those who don't use it. A nifty bit of creative accounting.

Project planners could have made better use of their *life experience*. They would have known about a similar light rail project in Edinburgh's CBD that took six years to build as engineers struggled with ancient sewer pipes in the historic city centre. The final costs exploded from GBP 375 million to GBP 776 million.

Decisiveness is an important property of decision-making. But a more rigorous use of decisiveness according to Nutt is the 'discovery process'. This seeks to uncover the concerns and considerations of stakeholders and engage in a process of networking and participation. It may take time, but it's more likely to result in a coalition of support due to the multiple smaller decisions made by everyone involved. And it's easier to resist competing or ill-conceived ideas being sold as a quick fix.

In the end, the trauma suffered by business owners in the central business district over seven years has never been compensated by the claimed social benefits of public transport. Had the planners approached the project with more *compassion* they might have seen the social, economic, and mental health costs in a more realistic light. Compensation could have been at the heart of the project rather than an after-thought.

It turns out that the idea imposition process is *four times* more likely to lead to the failure of a project than the discovery process according to Nutt.

Bad bankers

The Royal Commission into Misconduct in the Banking, Superannuation and Financial Services Industry was established on 14 December 2017 by the Australian Government. After seven rounds of public hearings, more than 130 witnesses, and over

10,000 public submissions Commissioner Hayne submitted a final report to the Governor-General on 1 February 2019 with 76 separate recommendations.

Reporting on the background to the Royal Commission, investigative journalist Adele Ferguson uncovered an unbelievable litany of widespread lying, cheating, and conniving over four decades in her 2019 book *Banking Bad*. When I read her book, I was living and working in Kuala Lumpur, Malaysia, where grand larceny is a national sport. Reading about my home country of Australia was humbling.

One of the biggest defences that came out of the Royal Commission was 'it's not me, it's the culture'. Individuals argued that they were not necessarily responsible. It was the culture of their organisation. 'Everyone was doing it.' But in what ways were those decisions thoughtful and considered, fair and just, in the short term and the long term? And which vested interests did they benefit?

Adele Ferguson writes about the terrible outcomes, the people who lost their jobs and the impact that had on their mental health and the mental health of their families. There are serious real-world ramifications for the decisions made by those bankers. And that's where system 3 thinking needs to be engaged. System 1 and 2 thinking will only take you so far, particularly where there is conflict between them.

For example, 'I need to do this because everybody else is doing it'. Or, 'why should I be the one who's marked out as being wrong?' It's too easy to think, 'there are systems in place where I can get away with it and my managers are protecting me, so I'll never get found out.' There's got to be a better way of parsing these attitudes for the benefit of the common good. That's where system 3 thinking comes in, to try to create some balance.

There's a tendency to demonise the players in this story and say, 'it's all narcissistic behaviour and greed'. Adele Ferguson's book gives the impression that the personality of the key players was at the crux of it. But personality and what else? Process. The report of the Royal Commission strongly advocated for a change in culture for those banking and insurance organisations. A change in culture is a change in the processes by which people engage one another, not just the mechanical business processes.

If you have a culture that supports system 1 thinking, you will find a more intuitive narrative. How can we make the most money? What feels good about how we serve the stakeholders? There's a lot of system 1 thinking and not much system 2 thinking, which is about risk, regulation, and compliance.

What the Royal Commission showed was that system 2 thinking was used by the players to try to cover up their mistakes and pretend it wasn't happening, to try to screen themselves from the regulators. This is not a good use of system 2 thinking at all. And where's the morality in that? As stewards of wealth, the bank is supposed to be serving the common good. But there was no system 3 thinking engaged by any of the key players.

The distinction is that system 1 thinking is what everybody else is doing. For example, suppose you are an operative in a bank. You're a mortgage processor or an insurance underwriter, whatever is in your job description. You're supposed to make money for the bank. Intuitively, system 1 thinking is carrying you along with the flow. System 2 thinking kicks in when you say, 'How can we get away with this? How can we cover this up? What justifies what I'm doing?' It's a post-facto rationalisation, where you realise that it's probably bad behaviour, but you can cover it up and get away with it.

System 1 thinking happens quickly, before you even know it. As an operator in that system, you could better engage your system 2 thinking by asking yourself:

- What's really going on here?
- How are our systems working?
- How do I calculate risk?
- What could go wrong?
- What is the future that I want for myself and for others?
- How do I do something about this?

This is why training in system 3 thinking should be a mandatory component of business decision-making processes to prevent this from happening again. The cost of reputational risk turns out to be a much higher price than any of the players in this drama admitted to.

The Boeing nosedive

When did the world's largest aerospace company lose its way?

On 29 October 2018, Lion Air Flight 610 crashed into the sea shortly after take-off from Jakarta, Indonesia. The plane was the latest version of the Boeing 737, a gleaming new 737 Max that was delivered just three months earlier – 189 lives were lost. On 10 March 2019, Ethiopian Airlines Flight 302 crashed into a field six minutes after take-off from Addis Ababa in Ethiopia, killing all 157 people on board. The plane was again a brand-new Boeing 737 Max. Within days, civil aviation authorities around the world issued grounding notices for the 737 Max. All 387 aircraft, which served 8,600 flights per week for 59 airlines, were banned from service by 18 March 2019.

Investigators found that a new automated flight control system, MCAS (Maneuvering Characteristics Augmentation System) malfunctioned on both flights, sending the aircraft into repeated nosedives. MCAS was designed to compensate for a design problem associated with mounting bigger engines on the old 737 airframe. Boeing had omitted the system from crew manuals and training. At the time of the Ethiopian Airlines crash, Boeing was aware of the faulty system and was in the process of releasing a software patch.

The decision to adapt the old 737 rather than design a new plane was driven by commercial and profit concerns. Boeing was in a desperate scramble to bring to market a new, more cost-effective aircraft to compete with its European-based rival Airbus, which was threatening to grab market share with its own next-generation planes. The company cut corners to get the plane out as quickly as possible. It used the least expensive suppliers, regardless of how inexperienced they were. And to make the 737 Max more attractive to airlines, Boeing said it required virtually no new training for pilots who were endorsed on its previous 737 models. It persuaded the US FAA (Federal Aviation Administration) and its airline customers that pilots didn't need costly flight simulator training to fly the 737 Max.

Boeing's problems go back to May 2001 when CEO Phil Condit and President Harry Stonecipher decided to move Boeing's corporate headquarters to Chicago, 1,700 miles away from Seattle where commercial aircraft assembly took place. Up until then, Boeing functioned as an 'association of engineers'. Its executives held patents, designed sophisticated flying machines, and shared a common language of engineering and safety. Finance wasn't the primary language.

But that changed with Boeing's takeover of McDonnell Douglas in 1997. New CEO Phil Condit signalled a culture shift from a preoccupation with technological breakthroughs to a focus on financial benchmarks. When Condit lost his job in a scandal over a US Defense Department contract in 2003, Stonecipher took over and transformed one of the most successful engineering cultures of all time into an image of GE, where Stonecipher had previously served. But with managers watching the numbers from Chicago and engineers reluctant to share their technical concerns in Seattle, it was a recipe for disaster. Stonecipher had his own career-ending scandal over a consensual relationship with an unnamed female Boeing executive in 2005, and his replacement was GE alumnus James McNerny. The level of estrangement reported among engineers, operators, and executives reached toxic levels. The company culture had sacrificed investment in engineering and safety for the bottom line. Dennis Muilenburg took over from McNerny in 2015. He was fired in December 2019 in the wake of the two crashes.

More disturbing than one poorly designed plane was the nose-dive of the culture at Boeing. 'This is a joke,' a Boeing employee reportedly said to a colleague about the 737 Max in 2016. 'This airplane is ridiculous.' Another employee wrote: 'I honestly don't trust many people at Boeing.' Internal documents show Boeing employees repeatedly questioning the competence of their colleagues and the quality of the company's engineering.

This is what happens when company culture is driven by system 1 thinking. In Stonecipher's case, this was his GE experience and the cost-cutting culture at McDonnell Douglas. 'I don't give 'em hell; I just tell the truth and they think it's hell,' he is reported as saying to engineers. Many CEOs superimpose their previous experience on their new appointments: *If it worked there it should work here*. But system 1 thinking at Boeing was the 80-year experience of relentless focus on safety and engineering. Culture is an emergent property of collective system 1 thinking. Experienced Boeing engineers found themselves sidelined and their concerns ignored by the new system 1 thinking encoded in slogans such as, 'a passion for affordability', and 'less family, more team'.

The clash of cultures was also evident in system 2 thinking. Boeing employees always knew they were an engineering-driven company, not a financially driven company. Cost-cutting and poor quality control to get the product out the door as quickly as possible was not in their DNA. But Stonecipher had the letters 'RONA' tattooed on his knuckles from his GE days: Return On Net Assets. His management philosophy was more returns, fewer assets. He planned to outsource as much of Boeing's business as possible. This would enable him to fire engineers, get rid of factories, and boost RONA. The stock price would go up, shareholders could cash out, and the board would be happy. A feat of financial engineering. But not great plane engineering.

What might have happened to Boeing if their CEOs had used more system 3 thinking to counter the imbalances between system 1 and 2 thinking?

- For a start, they would have recognised the strength inherent in the *diversity of values* and talent within the company.

- They might have been prepared to park their own *life experience* in order to listen and learn from the deep experience of the engineers at the core of the company's culture.

- Better *emotional regulation* could have afforded them a more inclusive dialogue in relation to the different claims from their employees, regulators, suppliers, and clients. Separating the headquarters from the main assembly areas revealed their ignorance of the emotional needs of employees.

- *Decisiveness* is a quality requiring moderation. Rushing decisions can be just as destructive as taking too long. The desperation to get the 737 Max onto the market to head off Airbus resulted in design and quality decisions being overruled.

- Where was *compassion* in the decision-making of CEO Dennis Muilenburg? It's necessary to question why Boeing didn't issue a grounding order as soon as they realised what had most likely caused the Lion Air crash. They knew. Yet they allowed the planes to keep flying while they worked on a fix, and 157 people who lost their lives in the Ethiopian Airlines crash might still be alive today.

- And finally, *focus*. Should companies focus mainly on profits? British economist John Kay writes in his 2011 book, *Obliquity: Why our goals are best achieved indirectly* about how the most profitable companies are not the most profit-oriented. Boeing originally created the most commercially successful aircraft, not through love of profit, but through love of planes.

After a year and a half of grounding, the 737 Max was finally cleared by the FAA to fly commercially in December 2020. Not only had MCAS been thoroughly re-programmed but other design flaws discovered during the re-certification process were also corrected. And yet Boeing continues to experience flaws with the 737 Max, the 787 Dreamliner, and the 777X. It seems they are yet to regain the engineering culture which was the hallmark of a successful aeroplane manufacturing company. System 3 thinking could have given them wings.

PRACTICAL STEPS FOR CHOOSING WISELY

Nobody has time. Everybody's rushing headlong into decisions. Decisions must be made, but there are costs involved with making quick decisions without due consideration. This notion of common good and fairness might seem unrealistic because there are too many competing interests and your decision depends on whose interests you serve. You might be a stakeholder or a shareholder in a business decision or in a political outcome, and perhaps you're tasked with serving the interests of the group that you're advocating for. Why would you be thinking about the interests of the other party when you've got to advocate for the interests of your own party? There is a natural tendency to create separation. But, as much as you can, think about the common interests: it makes negotiation a much deeper and richer experience, and the outcomes are likely to be more favourable for more people.

System 3 thinking has six dimensions to it. Set up a daily routine of checking your system 3 thinking. Ask yourself:

1. Am I focused?
2. Am I recognising my own life experience and how it plays out here?
3. Am I being decisive enough?
4. Am I exhibiting enough compassion and kindness?
5. Am I regulating my own emotional state?
6. Am I recognising and exhibiting tolerance for others' values and beliefs?

It's a way of reminding yourself to be switched on before you go into the day, otherwise you'll be operating on automatic with system 1 thinking. And that may not be the best place from which to make the most important decisions.

Facing challenges at work

Run through the six dimensions of system 3 thinking and realise which two or three are most relevant to the situation you face. For example, the dimension of compassion might turn out to be the strongest driver:

- Ask yourself, 'I've got to be compassionate to the people whose interests I'm serving. How am I helping families when I'm writing unnecessary insurance policies, and who is paying money that really shouldn't be paying? How is that right? Where's my compassion, and my compassion for my own family as well? How do I rationalise that?'

- Operating out of compassion creates a mental attitude which changes your approach to the thing that you're doing. That's how one of those dimensions of system 3 thinking might apply.

Go back to the previous chapter where I outlined the dimensions in detail and start to think through your dilemma, your doubts, and the potential for disruption. Think about what is actually at play here.

- The question you might ask yourself is, 'Why should I be the one who takes the fall? Nobody else seems to be bothered. Why is this bothering me?' That's the question that every actor in a bad situation has asked throughout history. 'Should I be the whistleblower? Should I be the martyr?'

- There comes a point, and this is where system 3 comes in, where someone has to act on behalf of the common good. If not you, then who? It does come down to the power of one.

Most businesses are set up with decision-making systems that are part risk mitigation, part avoiding error. There are a lot of decisions made on a day-to-day basis – big, weighty decisions involving many people's interests. You need to be careful and ensure that you're making the right decision. That's where system 3 thinking comes in.

Most business leaders don't apply system 3 thinking because they're only looking at the context of the decision within a business framework, not within a societal, community, and ecological framework. If you're a leader in an organisation you're charged with the authority to make those decisions and be responsible for them, so there's a lot more at stake.

Culture change is supposed to be driven by change management experts. They put the structures and frameworks in place for you to hang the cultural imperatives and cultural initiatives on. That's the way culture is supposed to change. But it never works that way because it can't be prescriptive. Culture is an organic process that emerges as a result of the people, the history, and everything else that surrounds what it feels like to work in that place. It can't be prescribed. It can't be mandated.

You change culture through the leadership walking the talk and expressing the behaviours they're looking for. For example, you can't advocate mask-wearing as the most important public health measure to protect everyone from a potentially deadly pandemic if you don't wear a mask yourself.

If everyone began to think about system 3 thinking in balancing system 1 and system 2 thinking, people would be more inclined to pause and think about how they might act in various situations. The standard approach is to be prescriptive and get everybody to do ethics training. Then you can tick the box. But after a while the same behaviours turn up. It's much better to find ways of engaging people where they are, to the point that they're making their own choices. That's where system 3 thinking can be most helpful. The idea of system 3 thinking is less prescriptive, but it becomes implicit in how you arrive at a decision.

Let's see if you're balancing this out correctly with a self-check on how well you are serving the common good:

- Am I focusing on this with the right approach?
- When I think about how others, such as my family, might view this and if I think about other people's experience, how do I sift this through the lens of life experience?
- Am I being decisive enough? I'm not just sitting on the fence, I'm moving forward quickly.
- Am I compassionate about the people who are involved in this decision?
- Am I regulating my own emotions and fully utilising whatever emotion is here? Am I recognising and identifying emotions without letting them overwhelm me or rule my decision?
- Am I recognising the different values that might be implicit in this decision?

You're never going to know in the moment whether you've made the right decision or not, but time will tell. People will tell you how foolish you were making that decision, but they'll come back and say, 'Well, you did make the right decision at the time.' Or it could be the other way around. This is not prescriptive in the sense that if you follow this approach you will always make the right decision. But you will move closer to making a wise choice on behalf of yourself and on behalf of the other interests involved – your family, your community. There's a higher probability that you will make a better decision.

You either make the decision that serves the interests of most people or you make the least worst choice in a situation where you are going to inevitably cause harm, striving to bring about the least harm to the fewest people.

If you're leading a business that is seeking to do the best it can for clients and for the community, and you believe that you're manufacturing a good product that is technologically effective and is going to benefit people, then it must, by definition, have some element of system 3 thinking in it.

The first thing to do in making any decision is to hit the pause button, then consider the information. System 3 thinking is almost supernumerary to decision-making. It's the essence, if you like. It's the culture within which the best decision can be made. If you apply the six dimensions of system 3 thinking, then you're applying the best elements of who we are as humanity to the decision, however that decision is framed. You're trying to move towards the decision outcome that's going to maximise the common good, or make the least worst choice under the circumstances.

Facing challenges at home

Imagine your partner in life is diagnosed with a life-threatening illness. What will you do about that? How do you approach it? Nothing will change the reality of the circumstances. Suppose you've got as much information as you can about the health of your partner and the prognosis doesn't look good. It's quite likely that your partner may in fact pass away within months or years. Your life course is about to change. How do you deal with that?

Developing a practice of system 3 thinking may help you cope with the situation:

- Being able to *focus* is number one. Being present for your partner, their suffering, and their needs while at the same time focusing on your own needs and suffering.

- Don't beat yourself up and think you're not caring enough. Be *compassionate*, be gentle with yourself, and offer as much compassion as you can to your partner.

- Be *decisive* about the things that matter. Don't let things go on for too long. If a decision needs to be made about starting this or that treatment, once you've given it due consideration just get into it. Don't delay.

- Be aware of the fact that your own emotions can get in the way. Practise *emotion regulation* by being honest with your emotions rather than getting hooked or caught up on particular feelings of anger and frustration. Realise those feelings are part of who you are and part of what makes your relationship with your partner what it is. Be prepared to have that kind of conversation.

- It's important to realise that what you value is perhaps different to what your partner values. What's important to them at that point in time is different to what is important to you. Recognise and do your best to *tolerate diversity of values*.

System 3 thinking could be a way of soothing what you're going through. It provides you with a template for traversing this deeper valley that you and your partner are crossing, something different to a spiritual or family frame of reference. There are no easy answers. There's not necessarily any happy ending, but there is a way in which you can manage your mental attitude and manage your approach to the situation.

Situations like this are not free from conflict. Perhaps your partner is going to die and you can't cope with having them at home. But they don't want to go into a care facility. There's not going to be a happy resolution, but you can explore the least worst choice.

Perhaps your partner doesn't want to move into care yet. What gives you the right to say otherwise? Who do you think you are? But if you consider the greater good and what's of maximum benefit for the most people involved in the situation, perhaps you are the right person to make the choice. You have the moral authority to do what you believe is right, provided you're making the decision using a system 3 thinking approach. You're seeking to maximise the good that can come out of the situation and to minimise the harm to the best of your ability. But you're also thinking from a broader perspective. You're thinking about it for the benefit of everyone whose interests are being served in this situation.

CONCLUSION

It's easy to be consumed by frustration, sadness, and despair when you consider all the foolish decisions being made in the world today. Maybe you want to be like Peter Finch playing Howard Beale in the 1976 film *Network*, throwing open the windows and shouting, 'I'm mad as hell and I'm not going to take this anymore!' It's easy to be completely demoralised. But if you understand how those decisions are made and how they could be improved, that gives hope for a better future.

We all face the implications of so many bad decisions made by so many leaders. How could that impact have been reduced? If those leaders had taken the time to apply different ways of thinking, could the outcome have been different? How can you apply system 3 thinking to achieve better outcomes for yourself, your employees, and the communities that you serve? While there's no guarantee that this will produce the right decision, I believe it will increase the probability of it being right. Not everyone will be happy, but it will produce a decision that's going to be more beneficial to more people.

WHAT'S COMING UP?

Next, I'll show you a useful template for quickly utilising System 3 thinking – the WISE Framework – and how you can use it to make more effective and wise decisions.

The WISE Framework for making better decisions

Pilots and surgeons rely on checklists to avoid disasters and make confident decisions. You need a checklist to help you make better decisions. That's the WISE Framework.

WHY YOU NEED A DECISION-MAKING FRAMEWORK

I shielded my eyes against the glare of the shimmering whiteness of the salt lake stretching from horizon to horizon. I was standing beside the Ford pick-up truck I had driven cross-country from the newly established mining town of Leinster on the edge of the Great Victoria Desert. My travelling companions were an American anthropologist from the Western Australian Museum and three full-blood first nation elders from the Pitjantjatjara group of Central Australia. It was March 1977. I was 23 years old and fresh out of university. As the newly appointed personnel research officer for Agnew Mining Company at Leinster, one of my tasks was to identify any sacred sites on the mine lease that would need to be avoided by construction activity. The previous evening, around the campfire as we ate freshly killed kangaroo tail, my companions told the dreamtime story of the rainbow serpent: how a man and a woman were chased from Uluru in Central Australia by the rainbow serpent across the western desert and finally out to sea near Carnarvon on the west coast. Growing up in Australia at that time, our primary school education was replete with these dreamtime stories. I always thought they were like nursery rhymes. But sitting there under the stars, listening to these elders tell the story, there was a surprising richness and complexity to it.

I had parked the truck at the top of an escarpment leading down to the shoreline of the salt lake. We had been following the path of the rainbow serpent. One of the elders pointed to a sand dune down by the shoreline and said, 'snake sleep there'. The sand dune was a conical shape, deep ochre in colour, about 10 metres high. The minerals in the sand had oxidised over thousands of years into stripes. And at that moment, I could see what looked like a tiger snake curled up asleep by the shore of this ancient salt lake. We drove down to the base of the sand dune and the elder pointed his finger at the featureless horizon and said, 'snake go there'. He was quite definite about where he was pointing his finger, but I couldn't make out any detail that might distinguish the direction he was pointing.

It took us two hours to drive around the outer shore of the salt lake to where he said the snake had been chased underground: a natural spring of water beneath a cleft of weather-beaten rocks. And straddling the rocks was a windmill pumping this water to the surface for the livestock of the local station owner. I suddenly realised what these stories were all about. They were remarkable navigation aids that these people could use to cross a feature-less desert. As a European I could only see desert and horizon. The Pitjantjatjara people could actually see where to find water. I wouldn't have survived out there more than a few days, but they have survived, generation after generation, because they know the story of the rainbow serpent.

And for me that early experience, fresh out of university and getting in touch with the local elders and the traditional owners of the land, led me to the work of helping people find streams in the desert, to actually help them to cross their desert and find some deeper source of meaning, and some way of making better decisions.

When you think about the situation that you're facing, whatever the decision is that you're about to make, what are you actually seeing? You might be seeing featureless desert, but you're not pay-ing attention to some other elements of the environment. There are things that you could be missing.

And that's why you need a decision-making template.

THE WISE FRAMEWORK

The WISE Framework is made up of the following four steps:

1. **Widen** your view
2. **Interrogate** the reality of the situation
3. **Sense** the future, which is different from gut feeling or intuition
4. **Enact** a way forward

Let's have a look at each of these.

1. How to WIDEN your view of the problem

We tend to think in binary terms; either/or, this/that. Time pressure generally pushes you into an A or B choice. It's much less effort to narrow your choices down to A or B than to consider extra options. But in complex decision-making, there are many more choices than that. You have to widen the way you're viewing the problem because you're looking at multiple variables.

In a form of psychotherapy called 'brief solution-focused therapy', there's the idea that the solutions to the problem exist in 'possibility land'. There are always many possibilities for you to explore. In the desert, I realised that the story of the rainbow serpent presented many more possibilities and that my choices weren't limited to 'should I go left or right?' I could go sideways. It's a different approach to thinking about the problem.

See beyond your horizons

In December 2003 I was appointed executive coach for Tim, head of mining and metals Asia Pacific for a European investment bank based in Sydney. Tim had started his career as a mining engineer in South Africa and progressed to become CEO of a gold mining operation in Western Australia. He decided to work in investment banking because he thought it might be fun. Actually, he had a much deeper reason. Tim had first-hand experience of how mining operations could either damage or benefit local communities. He resolved to find out how mining could be a force for good through the proper direction of financial resources. Soon after I began my journey with Tim he was promoted to global head of mining and metals. This meant he now had control of operations in Sydney, Singapore, Bangkok, Almaty, Delhi, Rio de Janeiro, Santiago, Toronto, Vancouver, Moscow, Amsterdam, and London.

Tim took to the air to meet all his staff and gain an understanding of the mining investments portfolio in each region. It was a punishing schedule criss-crossing the globe: 'If this is Tuesday then I must be in Almaty!' I noticed Tim was becoming exhausted and overwhelmed. In one of our coaching sessions reviewing his strategic plan I asked the naïve question, 'what would happen if there was no geography?' Tim was puzzled. 'If you took away the geography, how would you organise the business?' I asked. This was a light bulb moment for Tim. He jumped up to the whiteboard and started scrawling lines of communication between people and offices. He would stratify the business according to stages of business development rather than operational location. This meant three natural nodes – Singapore, Delhi, and London. Tim's widening of the possibilities for solving his problems gave him a springboard for growing the business. Soon afterwards he realised that Sydney was not in the best time zone for managing such a global business and he relocated his family to Amsterdam.

See what others see

Nizam was the CEO of a Malaysian financial guarantee insurer headquartered in Kuala Lumpur. In 2017 my colleagues and I from ICLIF (International Centre for Leadership In Finance) had been working with his executive team to improve leadership effectiveness and employee engagement. The board had agreed to pivot from covering large-scale financial transactions to dealing with small and medium enterprise businesses. This would mean more transactional services and fewer of the 'big deals'. Many key technical staff were unhappy about the changes.

By early 2018 after significant turnover it became clear that the unhappiness extended to the CEO. The executive team were split in their support of the CEO and a colleague who saw himself as the 'CEO-in-waiting'. With the support of the executive team I convinced Nizam that we needed to work one on one. I started our executive coaching engagement in mid-2018, and right away I could see Nizam held an idealised version of himself. He was deeply religious and committed to doing 'the right thing' by all concerned. By his own admission he was the 'reluctant CEO'. Many in the organisation appreciated his genuineness and his care. His top five character strengths were gratitude, spirituality, leadership, honesty, and authenticity. But Nizam procrastinated with decision-making. He would push for consensus or allow the parties to come to their own decision. This was intensely frustrating for his executive team who were in the midst of a business turnaround. Nizam could see this but he didn't know how he could be other than his authentic self. He was stuck.

It was only when I debriefed the results of a psychologically powerful 360-degree feedback report with him in early 2019 that he was able to widen his view. Suddenly he saw himself through the eyes of his executive team. It was a shock. I imagined how primitive tribespeople must have recoiled seeing their image in a mirror for the first time. Nizam's idealised picture of himself melted before my eyes. It took a while for him to compose himself. But then he generated deep compassion for his executive team and what they must have been going through. He began to recognise that he had responsibility as a CEO which did not invalidate his deep ethics. He realised that he possessed a much wider array of instrumental approaches to his role than he had previously allowed. As we continued to work together he started to act more decisively and communicate his vision for the organisation more deliberately. Widening his view of himself had given him access to the tools and resources to be the 'rightful CEO'.

🦉 Get WISE

The four critical questions that will widen your view

You can never have all the information you need to make a properly informed decision. It can be a waste of time trying to come up with lots of alternatives. But perspective matters. Looking at a problem from different angles does yield important insights. Sometimes the problem is startlingly clear, or sometimes you know how to solve the problem because it's in your specific domain of expertise. You already have the knowledge and skill and you can just go ahead and solve it. But for non-predictable and complex problems, it's important to consider the broader context within which the problem sits.

I've come up with four self-reflective questions that you should ask yourself at this time to help you widen your perspective:

1. Instead of 'either/or' or 'whether-or-not', what other options are there?

2. What is most important to me right now?

3. In what ways could my opinion be incorrect?

4. Who has solved this problem before? (Google it!)

2. How to INTERROGATE THE REALITY of the situation

We make assumptions and jump to conclusions so readily that the following question must be considered: 'Is the reality I'm seeing the same as the reality you're seeing?' You need to interrogate the reality of the situation that you see to understand what you are looking at.

The first step towards choosing wisely is seeing and accepting reality for what it is, not what you wish it to be. And this is vitally important. What are you seeing? It is what it is. That's the reality. It's not how you want it to be, it's just how it happens to be.

Not everyone wants you to succeed

When I met Anne in Sydney in late 2011, she had just taken up the position of Vice President, Customer Solutions, Marketing & Strategy, for a French/American global telco. She selected me as her executive coach, and we worked together for a year. Initially, Anne was facing clandestine sniping from some of her key technical support staff. And she wasn't getting the support she expected from senior management. Anne had a clear plan for how her division could deliver outstanding customer service and she assumed everyone would be on board, but no one was listening.

Why?

I encouraged Anne to interrogate her current reality before jumping into execution of her strategic plan. It turned out that she had supportive working relationships with some of her team but not with the key technical support group and not with her principal sponsors in other divisions. This was a surprise. Anne could see she needed to 'circle the wagons' to fend off arrows being fired by others outside her remit. Through analysing the strength and political significance of her relationships she was able to focus attention on stakeholder management. We worked on ways of having difficult conversations and influencing key individuals, cultivating a signature presence in management meetings, and doing more things on her own terms.

Towards the end of our engagement in 2012, Anne was appointed to the position of Vice President for the National Broadband Network, a nationally significant role and a recognition of her ability to get things done with a diverse coalition of stakeholders. She told me this wouldn't have happened if she had just accepted everything she was being told and expected everyone to support her. Anne's corporate success began with seeing things as they were, not how she imagined or wished them to be.

Look every gift horse in the mouth

A foreign currency scandal in 2004 caused one of Australia's 'big four' banks to lose more than $360 million and suffer significant reputational damage. An employee engagement survey in 2005 showed that staff were strongly connected to their customers but disengaged from the organisation. Subsequently, the bank commenced a three-year cultural transformation program which involved leadership development. In mid-2006, my colleagues and I from the Australian Institute of Executive Coaching co-designed and delivered a three-day residential leadership program for senior managers. This was followed by executive coaching.

One of my clients was Patrick, who was Regional General Manager for Corporate Banking. At the time the organisation was going through a vigorous restructure process. In early 2007, Patrick told me he had a dilemma. He was being offered the role of either head of investment banking or head of retail banking, both equally attractive to him. Which should he choose? He thought head of retail banking would be better for his career, although he was less familiar with the business.

I encouraged Patrick to fully investigate the reality of both positions. Who would he be working with? What would his executive team look like? What key results was he expected to achieve? What did he know and what didn't he know about both roles? I helped Patrick interrogate his assumptions and biases about the reality of the two roles. In late 2007 his decision was announced in the business press. He was the new head of investment banking. Soon after our coaching engagement finished, Patrick informed me that he had also been given a part of retail banking as well. His choice had led to a better outcome than he could have anticipated because he took the time to interrogate the reality of his options.

🦉 Get WISE

The four critical questions that will interrogate reality

Interrogating reality is similar to applying integrative thinking, which is how to take into account all of the different elements of the problem that might be occurring, both inside and outside of the frame of reference that you're using. In his book *The Opposable Mind* (2009) Roger Martin, Dean of the Rotman School of Management, University of Toronto, came up with a series of counterintuitive questions to help with integrative thinking and to get people to think differently about strategy.

Sometimes, too much analysis can lead to paralysis of decision-making. But it certainly helps to gather as much information as you can before trying to solve the problem. However, some problems may be impossible to interrogate because they exist beyond the realm of quantifiable data. Emotional states are a case in point. You can't readily interrogate an emotion, but you can think about a feeling. So, there are limits to how much you can interrogate reality.

Here are four self-reflective questions that you can ask yourself:

1. What would have to be true for each of these options to be the best possible choice?
2. What am I prepared to give up for this option to become a reality?
3. What's the biggest obstacle to this being the right choice?
4. In what ways could this response fail?

3. How to SENSE THE FUTURE you want to create

What is likely to emerge because of the problem? We tend to make decisions based on the fluttering of our emotions, whether it feels right or wrong. But sometimes there's a deeper meaning to the problem than might at first seem obvious.

Some decisions need to be made immediately. But thinking about the emergent property of something much bigger allows for a broader interpretation of the potential problem. You can start to see beyond your immediate horizon and start to think in a much more deeply felt way about what might be emerging from this problem.

It's true that most problems don't need to be sensed. Only when there are massive changes occurring can you step back and think about the emerging future state and what will become the new normal. In the midst of the COVID-19 pandemic, people were starting to talk about what will be on the other side, starting to sense the future emerging from the fear and grief.

When it doesn't make sense, don't do it

James was a rising star. As a consulting partner he had won the biggest single contract for Australia's largest professional services firm in 2015. As his executive coach I was helping him with his strategic thinking. James had a passion for transport. He and his team were steering an ambitious transformation program for Transport for New South Wales involving data management systems, integrated networks, customer experience, branding, marketing, and communications.

James could see the potential for a connected transport system. But he dreamed of something much bigger. He sensed an emerging future in the connected city, economically and socially, and he wanted to play a central role in bringing this to life. So, in early

2016 he hooked up with Google and IBM and organised a meeting in San Francisco to discuss a multi-million-dollar deal to develop the connected city of the future. However, his managing partner at the time insisted Google should pay for his airfare. James couldn't believe it. The potential revenue for the firm was a multiple of the biggest deal he had landed the year before. But now he was constrained by bureaucracy. He realised the organisation was not as invested in his vision as he thought. Soon afterwards, James left to go into his own start-up business. His sense of the future was stronger than his desire to play by the rules.

Look for signs that help you make sense

It was a clear tropical morning. The heavy rain over the past few days had left the grass quite sodden. I was standing by the pool area of the Cyberview Resort and Spa in Cyberjaya, Malaysia on 30 November 2018. It was the last day of a five-day residential leadership program for Associate Directors of the Central Bank of Malaysia. I had designed and co-facilitated this program along with my colleagues from ICLIF (International Centre for Leadership In Finance).

As participants wandered down for the usual morning yoga class, I told them we would be doing something different. 'Decision-making involves an element of sensing,' I said. 'Sensing is noticing the subtle messages pointing the way to your future.' I instructed the group to bring to mind a question they had around an important personal or professional decision. And, without thinking about an answer, they were to go 'walkabout' around the grounds of the resort. 'Let your feet carry you,' I said. 'Watch for signs and suggestions in the environment. You will sense the answer when you see it.' This was certainly a counterintuitive exercise for mid-career central bankers. But I knew they would dutifully follow my directions as the *Mat Salleh* (Malay for white Caucasian, derived from 'mad sailor', which is how Malays typically encountered Westerners in their early history). However, everyone seemed quite enthusiastic and they wandered off into the gardens and luxuriant foliage of the resort. Standing there alone, I thought perhaps I should do the exercise myself. What was I sensing about a decision I had to make? At that time, our centre was in the process of being acquired by the Asia School of Business, also an educational agency of the Central Bank of Malaysia under a legacy arrangement. Continuation of our contracts was in doubt. *What would I decide*, I thought, *if an offer was made to extend my contract … would I accept?* Just then I looked up as an airliner flew high in the sky above, its white contrail reflecting the morning sun. It was a beautiful sight. I noticed it was on a south-easterly bearing, overflying Peninsular Malaysia, probably flying to Indonesia, or further afield to Australia. The lyrics of the 1966 John Denver song *Leaving on a Jet Plane* played in my head. And then I sensed the answer to my question. No, I would not renew my contract. I was ready to go home.

🦉 Get WISE

The four critical questions that help you sense the future

There's a distinction between *intuition* and *sensing*. Sometimes they're confused, but they're not the same thing. Intuition is an experiential sense, a gut feeling. We're good at making intuitive decisions because we process a lot of information very quickly. But feeling good or not so good about the decision is not the same as deeply sensing what the likely future might be and imagining that future. Practising these questions can help you see what is likely to emerge on the other side of the problem:

1. In the current moment and looking forward to the next two to three years, what future do I want to create?

2. Where in my own being and in my environment can I find the seeds of the future now?

3. What is the essence of this issue? What is my deep knowing about this issue?

4. What might other people think or feel who are watching me make this decision?

How to ENACT A WAY FORWARD without procrastinating

It's possible to be too contemplative about a problem and not do anything about it. But one way or another, you need to take action. Goal setting is a well-established pathway for enacting a way forward for well-defined problems and scenarios. But for unpredictable situations, the best way to take action is through a series of experiments – pilots or prototypes to explore what will likely be the best action to take.

Act on the smallest details to the biggest picture

I had been Susan's executive coach in a previous role. Now, as the managing director of a national mortgage broking business she had brought me in again, this time to help her conceptualise the business, provide leadership development for the executive team, and manage growth. Business was rebounding from the Global Financial Crisis of 2008–10. Australia was experiencing a property boom, and banks and financial institutions were falling over themselves to meet the lending demand. I met Susan and the executive team in early 2014. The boardroom on level 34 of a prestige office tower in North Sydney commanded breathtaking views of the Harbour Bridge, the Opera House, the city, and the Pacific Ocean beyond.

Susan explained how the company was experiencing double-digit growth and they needed to scale the business. She wanted to make sure the executive team had a growth mindset and were prepared for the challenges ahead. Six months after that meeting staff numbers had doubled, and three months later they doubled again. The company acquired level 35, the top floor of the building, and Susan set about designing and refurbishing both floors. As the calendar rolled into 2015, Susan was managing design, construction and installation of the new office, the HR function, COO function, culture change and employee engagement, and marketing and branding. I continued to work with her on organisational design, selection and assessment, team development, and executive coaching. As exhausted as she was, Susan was a powerhouse of execution. She never wavered from her vision for the company, and she enacted the way forward from the smallest details to the bigger strategic picture. The company threw a lavish Christmas party for all staff and their partners that year at one of Sydney's premier harbourfront venues. Susan was publicly and privately congratulated for her efforts. And the company went on to become recognised as Australia's largest and most successful private mortgage broker a year later. Susan had prepared the way forward through her persistent action.

Set a clear intention as the first step

The Marble Bar dates back to 1893. The Victorian structure was painstakingly dismantled from the former Adams Hotel, transported and reassembled in the basement of the Hilton Sydney in 1973. Every detail of the façade of the restored mahogany bar and marble archways tells a story of the rich and famous who have graced her gilded hallways. That was where I met David for our first career transition coaching session, on 14 February 2020. An auspicious start, I thought. I had been David's executive coach since late 2011 when he was the MD of a brand marketing firm based in North Sydney. For the past three years he had been CEO of an Asia Pacific design agency. But now he was looking for a challenge. Over the next two months I helped him get clear on what he was looking for. But searching for a new job as the COVID-19 pandemic spread was never going to be easy. Once David compiled a list of contacts and firms with interesting approaches to market, he had to enact his search strategy. This meant having numerous e-coffee meetings and submitting his CV to everyone on the list who showed interest. With every meeting his intention became sharper. Taking action created momentum. Then, in June 2020 through a chance note on LinkedIn, the Australian chairman of one of the biggest brand marketing companies in the world contacted him. They were thinking of setting up a new division and he wanted David to head it up. Shortly afterwards, David resigned as CEO and prepared to start his new role. It was exactly in line with his most hoped-for position. He recognised that it wouldn't have happened unless he had enacted his clear intention. Perhaps it's true that 'life really is generous to those who pursue their destiny' as the Brazilian poet and lyricist Paulo Coelho wrote in his 1987 bestselling book *The Pilgrimage*.

Get WISE

The four critical questions that help you enact a way forward

This is what entrepreneurs do. They fail forward and fail fast. It's only through taking some kind of action that you learn what works and what doesn't. It's important to allow safe opportunities for people to play with ideas and make mistakes.

Most leaders would argue that it's costly to fail. However, contained prototyping is a proven approach to taking action and finding out what works. Present-day entrepreneurs know to fail forward, fail fast, and fail frugally. That cost is now taken into account.

Here are four questions to enact a way forward:

1. What can I start doing now?

2. What is an appropriate threshold for me to take action?

3. In what ways can I experiment or prototype these options?

4. What can I learn from this?

APPLYING THE WISE FRAMEWORK

The WISE Framework comes from my research and my executive coaching practice in developing a way to help people, teams, and leaders make better decisions. I've been using the WISE Framework for a while now and the people who use it have demonstrated an ability to make much better choices as a result. It's essentially a series of reflective questions. The same process operates for surgical checklists or for airline checklists. It's a very simple set of questions which help you to cover off on those areas that you might not otherwise be deliberately thinking about.

Your complete WISE Framework checklist of questions

Widen *your view to see many more possibilities*

1. Instead of 'either/or' or 'whether-or-not', what other options are there?
2. What is most important to me right now?
3. In what ways could my opinion be incorrect?
4. Who has solved this problem before? (Google it.)

Interrogate *the reality of the situation, not how you wish it to be*

1. What would have to be true for each of these options to be the best possible choice?
2. What am I prepared to give up for this option to become a reality?
3. What's the biggest obstacle to this being the right decision?
4. In what ways could this response fail?

Sense *the future, which is different from gut feeling or intuition*

1. In the current moment and looking forward to the next two to three years, what future do I want to create?
2. Where in my own being and in my environment can I find the seeds of the future now?
3. What is the essence of this issue? What is my deep knowing about this issue?
4. What might other people who are watching me make this decision think or feel?

Enact *a way forward by making a decision and acting on it*

1. What can I start doing now?
2. What is an appropriate threshold for me to take action?
3. In what ways can I experiment or prototype these options?
4. What can I learn from this?

Choosing wisely takes practice

It's an important principle of WISE decision-making that you need to create some space to contemplate or consider the elements of the problem. Procrastination can be a strategy to regulate the stress of the problem, but not making a decision is, in itself, a decision.

You need to be able to decide quickly, but the idea of using a framework like this is to give some space between the stimulus and the response, to give some thinking time. It's almost by definition that a WISE decision has involved some consideration and some thinking, even if that thinking has only happened within a few minutes, as opposed to a few weeks.

The WISE Framework gives you a tool to reduce decision-making errors which arise from biases, heuristics and logical fallacies, and increases the probability of making a wise choice.

It's no guarantee that you'll choose wisely when faced with doubt, dilemma, or disruption. What seems like a wise choice in the short term might not turn out to be so wise in the long term, and vice versa. But you're more likely to be assisted to make a wise decision using the framework than not using it. Apply the WISE Framework whenever you're approaching a big or difficult decision.

CONCLUSION

The WISE Framework is an elegant way of sifting the information you have before making a decision. Asking yourself these questions will take you outside of your biases, your logical fallacies, and your stereotypes. It can challenge your thinking sufficiently to enable you to make a wiser choice than you otherwise would have made. The idea behind this framework is that you apply it.

When you don't know what you don't know, sometimes sensing is all you can do when you're waiting for the emergent principles of the situation. But at least this framework gives you some guidance to know which direction to take. It acts as kind of compass.

In team decision-making, you might invite team members to adopt each of the W-I-S-E positions and really challenge each other, rather than jump to consensus. If you arrive at consensus too quickly, you might miss important information. And perhaps some of these questions will challenge that consensus.

For certain problems, some of these questions will really resonate and others won't be particularly useful. But just looking at this framework before you make a decision might remind you of one or two key questions that could prove incredibly valuable.

WHAT'S COMING UP?

The next chapter looks at the bigger picture and proposes ways to adapt yourself and others to the great turning wheel of history. What can we expect, in terms of where we're heading as a society? How can you wisely anticipate and prepare for the future? What do your decisions mean?

Creating a brighter future

You will face significant moments of choice in your life which may involve doubt, dilemma, or disruption. How you face such moments of choice will depend on how prepared you are. And right now, the world needs you to choose wisely.

THE GREATEST CITY IN THE WORLD

It is pre-dawn, mid-September 2018. We are following a procession of tourists and their guides across an ancient pathway in the dank tropical forest of central Cambodia. We emerge into an open field with a shallow lake at its centre. The surroundings are shadowy and indistinguishable. Our guide ushers us to a position beside the lake where we await the rising of the sun. Dawn is suffused by monsoon clouds, but in the grey light we see the famous silhouette of Angkor Wat with its pinecone-like towers. For the next few hours, we wander the massive halls and galleries of this lost city temple. It's surprising just how intact it is, despite crumbling sandstone blocks and black mould-draped walls. The bas-reliefs are exquisite. Every detail of construction is imbued with spiritual significance. It's difficult to comprehend the sheer scale of this place, reportedly the largest religious monument in the world by land area. Later, we stop in an antechamber to receive a blessing from a young monk – and to escape the cloying heat.

Our guide tells us that construction of the temple took place in the early 12th century during the reign of the Hindu King Suryavarman II. It was built as the king's state temple and capital city of the Khmer Empire. What a grand and shining city it must have been. Yet, just 27 years after the death of the king, Angkor was sacked by the Chams (present-day Vietnam). But Jayavarman VII ousted the invaders in a famous naval battle on Lake Tonlé Sap and was proclaimed king a few years later. He established a new capital and temple a few kilometres north of Angkor Wat. The new city, Angkor Thom, which encompassed Angkor Wat, was the largest pre-industrial city in the world. It supported an estimated population of one million people and covered an urban sprawl of almost 300 square kilometres. That's about the size of modern-day Los Angeles. This was made possible by sophisticated water irrigation technologies, including the diversion of a major river through the heart of the city.

At the centre is the famous Bayon temple, its Gothic towers decorated with huge stone smiling faces. We clamber over the steps and terraces of this crumbling edifice in the shimmering noon heat. The faces have a freakish ability to follow you with their gaze – sometimes level with your eyes, sometimes staring down from on high. Our guide suggests this was exactly the effect King Jayavarman VII wanted to achieve as the Khmer Empire's most powerful ruler. He was a prolific builder, constructing roads, hospitals, walls and temples during his 37-year reign. We visit nearby Ta Prohm temple, constructed in the early 13th century, one of the most visited complexes in the Angkor region. Huge trees and vines thread the ornate ruins. We weave carefully through stone galleries, tilting dangerously. Silk-cotton trees and strangler figs devour the intricate architecture like giant aliens. This is the evocative scene for the movie *Lara Croft: Tomb Raider*.

Angkor thrived as the city centre of the Khmer civilisation for nearly 250 years until it was invaded and plundered by the Ayutthaya Kingdom (present-day Thailand) in 1431 CE. The Khmers abandoned Angkor and moved their capital further south-east to the site of present-day Phnom Penh. Angkor Wat was largely neglected but continued to be visited by Buddhist pilgrims through the 16th and 17th century. Eventually, the jungle swallowed up all traces of the once vainglorious Khmer city until it was effectively rediscovered by the French naturalist and explorer Henri Mouhot in 1860.

By late afternoon, we are overwhelmed by the babble of voices written in the stones of this ancient civilisation. Too many temples and not enough time. We gratefully retreat to our comfortable hotel in downtown Siem Reap.

THE COLLAPSE OF CIVILISATIONS

All civilisations rise and fall. Yet, at any point in time the fabric of daily life appears stable and unchanging. The human mind is not equipped to perceive incremental change. We fail to see the great turning wheel of history. The Fall of Angkor to the armies of the Kingdom of Ayutthaya in the 15th century was the defining moment of the collapse of the Khmer empire. But for decades before the invasion the city was struggling with overpopulation and deforestation. The resources needed to clear sediment from the canals was proving too much. Eventually, intense monsoon rains after a prolonged drought caused widespread damage to the city's infrastructure, leaving it vulnerable to attack.

Could our own civilisations of the early 21st century be primed for collapse? I believe there is a change of empire going on at this present stage of our history. We're seeing a widespread rise of populism and polarisation, fostered by social media platforms that are narrowing our views and interactions. We're witnessing the corruption of democratic ideals and the self-serving decisions that are being made for vested interests. And there is real, tangible evidence that our species may not survive because of what we're doing to the planet. Now, more than ever, we need leaders to make wise choices. Without wisdom, we're all going to suffer.

The COVID-19 pandemic was active during the writing of this book. It was not so much the virus that was the problem, rather it was the foolishness of people and how they reacted and behaved throughout the pandemic. Their behaviour and actions were arguably more dangerous than the virus itself. We seemed to be reverting to stupidity as our lowest common denominator. People protested mask-wearing and lockdown measures because they felt it was a violation of their freedom. But these public health strategies were the only available means to prevent rapid escalation of the virus. It wasn't a process of needlessly restricting civil liberty: it was the best available option to protect people for the common good. Yet, social media became an echo chamber for conspiracy theories which proliferated and flourished. That's the society we live in now, and it's a very dangerous time in our human history.

IS IT HARDER TO BE WISE NOW?

Everything is being challenged. There's widespread distrust of science, business, government institutions, politics, and news outlets. More people get information from their devices than from newspapers. Traditional media companies have always had to check their facts and abide by codes of conduct or face hefty fines. But the social media platform owners like Facebook (WhatsApp, Facebook Messenger, Instagram), Alphabet (Google, YouTube), Tencent (QQ, WeChat and QZone), Amazon (Snapchat), and Twitter have lagged in their willingness to check the veracity of posts or censor incivility (rude, aggressive, disrespectful, or offensive communication). Their excuse has always been the protection of free speech and open sharing. But if their algorithms incorporated fact-checking and blocking of hyper-polarising or extremist language they would likely lose income. A lot of income.

Governments have also lagged in their willingness to impose regulations for fair as well as open exchange. The horse has well and truly bolted from that stable. Conspiracies and memes have gone viral through platforms like 4chan, 8chan, 8kun, Endchan and the Dark Web. 'Pizzagate' emerged during the US Presidential Election in 2016 with its ludicrous claims of a child-sex ring run by Democrats out of a Washington pizzeria. By 2017 this gave rise to the fringe far-right conspiracy QAnon, which claimed a 'deep state' plot against US President Donald Trump led by Satan-worshipping elites from within government, business, and media. Yet, Twitter, Facebook, and TikTok only began banning lurid and false allegations of paedophilia and other crimes posted on their platforms by QAnon in late July 2020. By then QAnon believers had been linked to armed standoffs, riots, attempted kidnappings, harassment, and murder. The insurrection against the democratic declaration of the

US election results at the Capitol building in Washington DC on 6 January 2021 revealed just how dangerously fantasy can spill over into reality.

George Orwell showed remarkable prescience in his dystopian book *1984* (written in 1948): 'Not merely the validity of experience, but the very existence of external reality was tacitly denied by their philosophy. The heresy of heresies was common sense.' Ours is an era where common sense is flatly denied. There are facts and there are 'alternative facts'. Lies become truth and truth is drowned by the voices of hatred and vilification.

The American historian Barbara Tuchman (1912–89) describes the turning wheel of history from Troy to Vietnam. The key moments of choice were ones in which the 'wooded-headedness' of leaders prevailed. 'Wooded-headedness,' she says, 'consists in assessing a situation in terms of preconceived fixed notions while ignoring or rejecting any contrary signs. It is acting according to wish while not allowing oneself to be deflected by the facts'. Tuchman references Count Axel Oxenstierna, Chancellor of Sweden (from 1632–44), who is quoted as saying to his son on his deathbed, 'Know my son, with what little wisdom the world is governed'. He knew that back in the 17th century. It seems just as true today.

American archaeologist and historian Joseph Tainter applies network theory, energy economics, and complexity theory to explain the collapse of civilisations over a 2,000-year period. The ultimate cause of collapse is an economic one, he says. Civilisations grow in complexity as they solve problems. Complexity builds and builds, usually incrementally, without anyone noticing how brittle it has become. The cost of maintaining increasing social complexity eventually becomes prohibitive without additional inputs. Monumental architecture, artistic and literary support, and burgeoning bureaucratic institutions gradually exceed the resources available to pay for them. 'It's a classic "Alice in Wonderland" situation,' Tainter says. 'You're running faster and faster to stay in the same place'. Then some little push arrives, and the society begins to fracture. The result is a 'rapid, significant loss of an established level of sociopolitical complexity,' Tainter says. He points to the diminishing marginal rates of return on investment in energy, education, and technological innovation today as signposts of impending collapse – perhaps not immediately, but within the next few decades.

Russian-American biologist Peter Turchin is a professor of ecology and evolutionary biology, anthropology, and mathematics at the University of Connecticut. He uses complexity science software to find patterns in large historical datasets. He and two anthropologists at the University of Oxford launched Seshat, a database of historical and archaeological information named after the ancient Egyptian goddess of record-keeping. 'One truth that Seshat demonstrates,' Turchin says, 'is that, along with many unique milestones that were reached in different places and times, there are plenty of immutable patterns in our shared history. The more things change, the more they stay the same. And nothing makes this fact clearer than a close look at the data'. Turchin has been able to demonstrate a pattern of secular cycles in the societies that evolved into modern-day France and Russia from the first millennium BC until roughly 1800. He also showed that there were shorter oscillations in the stability of these societies, lasting about 50 years, which he called 'fathers-and-sons cycles': one generation set out to redress the injustices of the previous one, often violently, and the next shrank from violence having grown up with its aftermath. The third generation started it all over again. Using mathematical modelling, Turchin has developed predictive empirical patterns with a high degree of accuracy. In 2010 he predicted that mounting political instability would peak in the US and Western Europe around 2020. He pointed to climbing wealth inequality and public debt in Western nations, indicating that these societies were approaching a period of upheaval.

The Strauss-Howe Generational Theory was proposed by American playwright and theatre Director William Strauss (1947–2007) and American demographer and social researcher Neil Howe in the early 1990s. They realised that there were permanent differences in generations, and there was a recurring pattern going back to the 17th century in European and Anglo-American history. According to Strauss and Howe, a generation lasts about 20 to 25 years and ends in a 'turning'. Four turnings together constitute a cycle of around 80 to 100 years, which lasts from crisis to crisis. In the current era, the first turning occurred in the late 1940s and lasted until the 1960s. With reference to Anglo-American society, this was a time characterised by strong institutions and a solid consensus of where society wanted to go. The second turning during the 1960s and 1970s was when the Baby Boomer generation came of age. People wanted to shed conformity and civic responsibilities. The third turning from the late 1980s to the early 2000s was an 'unravelling'. Institutions were despised and untrusted and people lost faith in civic organisations. According to Strauss and Howe we are now in the fourth turning, which is the crisis era. This started in 2008 with the Global Financial Crisis and will extend through until 2030, although the 2020s will be the climactic decade. Fourth turnings tend to be driven by wars. The last fourth turning in American history was in the 1930s with the Depression and then World War II.

At this stage in our global history (the early third decade of the 21st century) we seem to be led by wooden-headed leaders who are intent on following the 'march of folly' according to Tuchman. To start the next turning of history requires 'grey champions' to plant the seeds of wisdom for the next generation, according to Strauss and Howe.

Are you one of them?

PLANTING SEEDS OF WISDOM IN A FIELD OF IGNORANCE

Ignorance has been around for a long time – for as long as there have been people. But today there are many more ways in which you can enact whatever your point of view is. The internet is wonderful in terms of freedom, but it can also be deliberately harmful in terms of its impact. There are increasing questions about the safety of the internet and whether we should step away from it and use private networks for things that matter – protecting our infrastructure, protecting our democracies. Perhaps we've given far too much openness and freedom to the internet and it's now coming back to bite us.

Some would argue, as American management consultant Margaret Wheatley has in her 2017 book *Who Do We Choose to Be? Facing reality, claiming leadership, restoring sanity* that 'we can no longer solve the global problems of this time at large scale levels'. It seems that poverty, economics, climate change, and violence to humanisation are out of our hands now. We need to be willing to use whatever power or influence we have to create islands of sanity that evoke and rely on our best human qualities to create, produce, and persevere. What does that island of sanity look like for you?

Is it your family? Is it your community? Is it a cluster of like-minded individuals that you feel compelled to protect? Future generations will cultivate those ideas that are germinating now. Creating islands of sanity preserves those seeds – the best of humanity – so that they will grow in the future.

To turn that around and start evolving again, we need to run our decisions through the filter of WISE decision-making. This is where system 3 thinking really comes in. As you face the entrenchment of stupidity and ignorance, ask yourself these questions: What seeds are you planting? What do you *focus* your attention on? What do you sense about the emerging future? Where do you see divisive polarisation and populism?

Pay attention to current affairs. Use your own *life experience* to assess what's happening around you. What seems sensible and reasonable to you? If you can make a positive difference in somebody's life then make that difference. Be *decisive*. Realise that *compassion* is what drives us forward. Compassion is how we evolve. How can you incorporate compassion, and how can you help others to take on a more compassionate view?

Acknowledge that these current circumstances can arouse incredible feelings of anger and frustration and fear. How do you *regulate your own emotions*? How can you use those emotions in a positive and productive way? Anger can be a force for good if you can direct it effectively. How do you tolerate – and make peace with – others who have *views and values so divergent* from your own? How can you see things from their perspective to be able to interpret what's happening in front of your eyes?

Here's how you can plant seeds of wisdom through the six elements of system 3 thinking:

- **Focus:** Notice what's going on in the world around you and pay attention, no matter how grim, distasteful, or unfair it looks. Don't turn away but don't become drawn in. Be a detached observer.

- **Life experience:** Draw on lessons from your own life and the experiences of others to see events and issues in the context of human development over a longer timeframe than what the news cycle or other people might be giving you. Take the opportunity, if you can, to advise those who seek guidance and wise counsel. Build up the practice of helping others.

- **Decisiveness:** If you can make a positive difference in another's life or in a community, then take action. Don't delay. Decide on the issues that matter to you and take a stand. Be known for your position.

- **Compassion:** Use your feelings of frustration, anger, sadness, and empathy to reach out and help those in need with whatever resources you have available at the time.

- **Emotion regulation:** Strive for balance in your emotional experience; identify your feelings and be honest about owning them. Don't be overwhelmed or confused. Notice your emotional state as a by-product of the issues that you're seeing in the world. But try to remain detached.

- **Tolerance for divergent values:** Develop and maintain a state of equanimity – calmness and composure – especially in a difficult situation. Have a level of curiosity about the issues and circumstances in the world. Try to imagine what other people might be feeling, even if their values and beliefs are diametrically opposed to yours.

Use the frameworks that I've been referring to all the way through this book – begin to apply them. What's the bigger picture? Reflect on the experience of repeating patterns in your own life and the experiences of others. When has this happened before? What have others done in the past to move out of these cycles?

Review your decisions in the light of longer-term events and circumstances. When is the right time to move out of or into the stock market? How safe and sustainable are your long-term living arrangements? Do you live above the predicted future sea level? Should you trust in God, but build on a hill?

Look for signs of genuine compassion and action that you can take during world events. How can you support and promote compassion in your life and the lives of others? How can you sustain your island of sanity?

Recognise your feelings of anger, fear, and despair, and seek to balance your emotional state with simple practices of equanimity and tolerance for divergent values. See how the cycles of history are reflected in current affairs and play out along the lines of deep and sometimes ancient religious, cultural, and tribal stories.

You're not alone. We all want to run away and hide sometimes.

Andy

Andy was a vagrant. He would sit on a park bench right on the waterfront of our Sydney harbourside suburb from sunrise to sunset, gazing out across White Bay towards Balmain. He wore the same clothes every day. He never showered, and he reeked as he passed by, tottering unevenly. Yet, he must have been aged only in his mid to late 30s. He would just sit there, day after day, in one of the most affluent suburbs in Sydney. Occasionally someone would give him a bag of chips, a bottle of soft drink, or buy groceries for him. He used to relieve himself in the garden of the apartment of a well-known Australian publisher. He was tolerated. People tried to move him on, but he never did move on. In winter, he would sleep under the eaves in front of the real estate agent's office, with window advertisements of million-dollar properties. This went on for years.

And then one winter morning in 2014 he collapsed and died of a heart attack – in our street. The whole community came out to celebrate Andy's life in a service held at the front of the real estate agent's office. Hundreds of people attended. A plaque saying 'Andy sat here' was put on his favourite park bench.

Nobody ever knew where he came from. He had no known relatives. Nobody could trace his whereabouts or his background. But he made such an impact on our community. We all felt a greater sense of connectedness. We took the effort to stop and chat to each other in the street, and small acts of kindness and compassion became commonplace in our affluent harbourside suburb. It made me realise the profound ripple effects that our lives have on the lives of others. If a vagrant could have such an impact, imagine the influence your life has on the many hundreds and thousands of lives you have touched.

That bench dedicated to Andy is still there.

That's fundamentally what this book has been about. It's about the choices you make and the impact of those choices. You may not know whether it's a wise or a foolish choice until sometime later, even years later– the ripple effect impacts so many others. That is why it's important to cultivate a wise practice for everyday life.

We are all participants in this long arc of human history, and it is wise to recognise patterns as they unfold and take wise action to protect ourselves from risk and to try to make the world a better place today and in the future.

Developing a practice of wisdom

Wisdom is a way of understanding the world. It's about seeking the ultimate causes and effects of events. It's a virtue and a personal good – intrinsically rewarding and something to be sought after. It is a human resource that is involved in many facets of successful human development. It applies not only to our lives as individuals, but to societal functioning. It refers to time-tested universal knowledge that guides our behaviour.

Wisdom is the integration of the emotional, intentional, and cognitive aspects of human abilities in response to life tasks and problems. It's a balance between the opposing interests that we find, and it relieves us from intense emotional involvement. It allows us to detach and to match our actions to what is going to be in the best interests of all concerned. It involves both our intelligence and our creativity, as well as our knowledge. Wisdom, by its very definition, should not be used towards the achievement of dark ends but to achieve a common good. Wisdom is a unique, complex, multi-component human trait. It involves dynamic and balanced integration of various components. It's greater than the sum of its parts. It's purposeful. It seeks to enhance the wellbeing of the self and of society.

My definition of wisdom is:

The conscious engagement of system 3 thinking (focus, life experience, decisiveness, compassion, emotional regulation, and tolerance for divergent values) to achieve the maximum good or the least harm for the most people and for society at the moment of choice.

To develop a daily practice of wisdom, apply the six dimensions of system 3 thinking through the lens of the WISE Framework:

- Widen your search for information beyond your own biases, integrating available data points as completely as you can.
- Sense what is emerging and what you wish for as the best and most ethical outcome among competing interests.
- Make a series of smaller decisions and experiment with what will work best for the common good in the short term and the long term.
- Take a stand on important issues. If you don't stand for something, you'll fall for anything, as the saying goes.
- Deliberately comment on current affairs, and articulate your opinions and views, drawing from your knowledge and experience.
- Practise cultivating emotional balance through articulating what you're feeling without those same feelings overwhelming you. Learn to recognise what and who presses your emotional hot buttons and take a third-person perspective on what appears to be unfolding, without taking it personally.
- Take a curious interest in other cultures, ideals, and beliefs as a way of enriching your perspective. Indigenous cultures have much to teach us in terms of the basic conditions for living in harmony with the planet, and with ourselves.
- Practise the skills of the compassionate mind: mindful preparation, mind training through imagery, forgiveness, and compassionate behaviour. These are all suggestions that British

clinical psychologist Paul Gilbert makes in his 2013 book *The Compassionate Mind: A new approach to life's challenges.*

You might say, 'Well, I can live a fulfilling life without needing to be wise. Surely, I can be happy. I don't need to be wise to live a meaningful life.' In the short term, we are engaged in a struggle between the profane and the divine. We're invited to realise our highest and purest being as an expression of the divine, but for most of us, the invitation is lost in the post. As American Franciscan friar Richard Rohr puts it, 'wisdom is the highest expression of human development'. Why not seek it?

The wisdom of pain

The Mugumo fig tree at Uhuru Gardens in Nairobi was planted by Jomo Kenyatta, the first President of the Republic of Kenya, in June 1964. It was planted at the same spot where the British Union Jack was brought down, and Kenya's national flag was first hoisted.

During the five-day Leader's Quest program in September 2016 I sat in the cool of that tree on a dry, hot afternoon to listen to readings by the celebrated Kenyan poet, playwright, and activist Sitawa Namwalie. In 2014 she had won Kenya's Sanaa Theatre Award for her show of dramatised poetry called *Silence is a Woman*, which also received the award for Best Production on Women's Rights and Gender Based Violence. I recall how elegant and wise she appeared. Statuesque and confident. Her head shaved, wearing opalescent earings and a blue, white, and lime-green striped African shawl.

After her readings she sat on the dry grass with us to answer questions. Knowing a little of her suffering, I asked her about the meaning of pain, referencing the pain I had experienced losing my family. 'It is an incredible honour to feel pain,' she said.

'These terrible things are all part of life. Just don't be overwhelmed. Whatever it is, it's your thing, it's your business. Don't expect others to be as passionate about it as you are. No one else can own it. It's yours.'

Walking back to our bus back to the hotel, I reflected on the wisdom of pain in Sitawa's life and in my own. 'You talk about what wisdom is, not what it feels like,' Gene, our Quest leader, challenged me. 'What's preventing you from knowing?'

I stammered that I didn't know. 'I think you do,' he said. 'I see wisdom in you already. You're not letting it out.' *What is the wisdom in me?* I wondered. What do I know, and why am I inhibiting myself from its expression?

Understanding the psychology of wisdom has shown me that we all possess wisdom-related resources to a greater or lesser extent. Most of us just don't know it. Not until we are faced with our own pain. Then we must find those resources to rise above the suffering. I saw in Sitawa's grace that she had found wisdom through her pain. And I was still struggling to articulate it.

The wisdom of wisdom

I am sitting on a massive shard of limestone rock jutting out over the valley 300 metres below. It's a hot and hazy afternoon. Typical conditions for Rajgir in North East India. It is 12 February 2012. We have walked the pilgrim's trail to the top of Vulture's Peak. This is the place where The Buddha gave his most significant discourses more than 2,500 years ago. Here he taught the Transcendent Perfection of Wisdom 16 years after his enlightenment, to an assembly of 5,000 monks, nuns, and laity, as well as innumerable bodhisattvas. On the way up the mountain, we stopped at several caves where The Buddha meditated. These rocks, worn smooth from millennia of devotees, once hosted the real Siddhartha Gautama, the actual Buddha Shakyamuni.

It feels as if I have come face to face with him here on Vulture's Peak. Astonishingly, what he taught has much in common with the modern sciences of quantum physics, cosmology, and psychology, particularly on the nature of the interconnectedness of all phenomena. For example, The Buddha claimed the idea of a fixed self is an illusion. And modern brain and behavioural scientists would agree with him about there being no evidence of an essential core, indivisible identity. We only exist – conventionally speaking – through the stories we tell about ourselves. Like modern biologists, The Buddha held that all things are in a state of flux: life is growth and decay, all phenomena arise and dissipate, everything is impermanent, and nothing can be truly relied on in and of itself. The Buddha's idea that nothing exists as an independent entity but rather arises through multiple causes and conditions is a fundamental tenet of ecology. Finally, he maintained that wisdom is the only antidote for gaining freedom from suffering.

And sitting there, at Vulture's Peak, on that afternoon in 2012, I suddenly felt that my rational scientific training was inadequate to explain my personal experience of The Buddha during our pilgrimage. Perhaps wisdom is ineffable after all. And yet I believe we must strive to make wiser choices in life, otherwise foolishness prevails.

CONCLUSION

I hope that by now you've learnt how to discern the differences between wisdom and foolishness, truth and deception, bias and reason, selfishness and generosity, and delusion and reality. Perhaps you're waking up to the reality that our civilisation today is on the verge of collapse. You can only do what you can with what you have, where you are, and establish an island of sanity amid the sea of madness.

Wisdom is the highest expression of human development. The choices we make in life are important. In the end, life is a summation and the product of all the choices we make. So, try to make wise choices.

See yourself as a significant part of the story of human history – because you are. Choose to be an active participant rather than a passenger. Take a philosopher's view of the bigger picture and the ultimate meaning of it all. We live out our brief lives clustered together on a unique – as far as we know – small blue dot in the unfathomable coldness and emptiness of the universe. How should that shape our view as a species?

I hope that now you'll consciously and deliberately establish a practice of wisdom for everyday life.

WHAT'S COMING UP?

Now it's over to you. Will you accept the invitation to establish your own island of sanity and sow the seeds of wisdom for future generations? You are a unique being in the cosmos and you do make a difference to others, in both small and significant ways. This is now your moment of choice.

Conclusion
Your moment of choice

The most important thing in developing a practice of wisdom
is to pay attention. Don't ignore what's happening around you.
Pay attention, listen, and keep an open mind.

There are plenty of reasons to be fearful and alarmed about the
condition of our world. Perhaps these are unique conditions in
human history. Or perhaps they're the same wicked problems
occurring over and over. But they're certainly calamitous in many
respects. We need to be prepared for the changes that are swirling
all around us. At a personal level, you can't control what happens
to you in life, but you can control your thinking, what you believe,
what your values are, and what choices you make.

I hope this book has given you the opportunity to be better
prepared and more confident facing significant moments of choice
in your life. The world needs more people like you to make wise
choices. This book will get you prepared to be one of those who
can help us out of this mess. There is a desperate need for wisdom

right now. I hope I've been able to distil the essence of wisdom down to what you can do and how you can be at any moment of choice. I want you to think, act and decide wisely with all the resources I have shared with you in this book.

Wisdom is observing what's happening around you and responding to the people directly in front of you. People who are in your group or in your particular enclave. And doing something to help them. That's ultimately what I hope this book will do for you. I'm confident you'll never again shy away from a moment of choice or let someone else make a choice for you. You are in control of your life, and I want you to have the confidence to make those choices that are important to you, no matter what other people might think.

You can now identify the most common biases you've experienced in the past and how you can avoid them in the future. Your reflection should help you to counteract the effect of these biases. When you're facing a moment of choice, remember to pause, step back, and think about the decision before committing to a course of action. Apply the WISE Framework when you're in doubt, facing a dilemma, or experiencing disruption. Become familiar with the questions to ask yourself and others as you or people around you prepare to make a big decision. This framework now becomes a checklist of how to improve the safety and reliability of your decision-making.

You can practise the six dimensions of system 3 thinking to figure out and sense what's going to be the best outcome for your wellbeing and the wellbeing of those around you, in both the short term and the long term, and for the greatest social good. This is how you curate a meaningful life for yourself without the expectations that other people have about you.

Review your results from the T3 profile and choose the most important dimensions to develop. Follow the suggested practices to raise your awareness of system 3 thinking and when to apply it. Consider a significant issue that you're facing now, or that you're going to face in the near future and create an action plan to better prepare yourself to make a wise choice. What do you need to do to prepare for that decision?

You might not be facing a moment of choice right now, but there is a very high probability that you're going to face tough decisions in the not-too-distant future. We all do. These are likely to be decisions you could not have predicted. That's when you're going to need this book. Use it to develop your wisdom resources now so that you'll be better prepared when that moment arrives. But if you are facing a tough decision now, this book will help you better prepare for it and increase the likelihood that you'll choose wisely.

In her 1999 book *The Cost of Living: The greater common good and the end of imagination*, Man Booker Prize–winning Indian novelist Arundhati Roy wrote about how to gain wisdom in the face of life's pain, injustice, and suffering:

> *To love, to be loved, to never forget your own insignificance.*
> *To never get used to the unspeakable violence and the vulgar*
> *disparity of life around you.*
> *To seek joy in the saddest places.*
> *To pursue beauty to its lair.*
> *To never simplify what is complicated or complicate what is simple.*
> *To respect strength never power.*
> *Above all to watch.*
> *To try and understand.*
> *To never look away.*
> *And never, never to forget.*

To me, that is an elegant distillation of what it means to choose wisely. That no matter what is going on around you, keep looking, keep searching, and don't turn away.

My greatest wish for you is that you never forget the light of wisdom shining within you. You have your own wisdom resources. They've always been there. I want you to nurture this light because it becomes a beacon of the best of human qualities for those around you and for the world.

There are more resources to help you choose wisely here **www.peterjwebb.com** where you can take the T3 profile. And by all means, contact me directly via the website for decision-making programs, consulting, or coaching.

Bibliography

Introduction: Moments of choice

The discovery of system 3 thinking

Webb, P.J. (2005). Inspirational Chaos: Executive Coaching and Tolerance of Complexity. In: Cavanagh, M., Grant, A.M., and Kemp, T. (Eds.). *Evidence Based Coaching (Volume 1): Contributions from the Behavioural Sciences.* Bowen Hills, QLD: Australian Academic Press.

Webb, P.J. (2007). Coaching for Wisdom. In: Grant, A.M., & Cavanagh, M.J. (Eds.), *Evidence-based Coaching Volume Two: Resources from the 2003–2007 Sydney Conferences.* (CD-ROM), Sydney NSW, CPU Press.

Webb, P.J. (2007). The Wisdom of Coaching. In: Church, M. (Ed.), *Ideas: Original perspectives on life and business from leading thinkers – Volume 2* (pp. 103-107), Seaforth, NSW, Thought Leaders Limited.

Webb, P.J. (2008). Coaching for wisdom: Enabling wise decisions. In: D.B. Drake, K. Gørtz, and D. Brennan (Eds.) *The Philosophy and Practice of Coaching.* San Francisco, CA: Jossey-Bass.

Kahneman, D. (2011). *Thinking, Fast and Slow.* New York, NY: Farrar, Straus and Giroux.

Chapter 1: How your choices get hijacked

Jumping to conclusions

Eagleman, D. M. (2011). *Incognito: the secret lives of the brain.* Melbourne, VIC: The Text Publishing House.

Bias

McRaney, D. (2012). *You Are Not So Smart: Why your memory is mostly fiction, why you have too many friends on Facebook. And 46 other ways you're deluding yourself.* Oxford, UK: Oneworld Publications.

Popper, K. (1999). *All Life is Problem Solving.* Oxford, UK: Routledge.

The effect of social media

Kaspersky Lab (2015). *From Digital Amnesia to the Augmented Mind.* Kaspersky Lab, 1st Floor, 2 Kingdom Street, London, W2 6BD, UK.

Griffiths, M.D. (2014). Adolescent Trolling in Online Environments: A brief overview. *Education and Health.* 32(3), 85-87.

John, A., Glendenning, A.C., Marchant, A., Montgomery, P., Stewart, A., Wood, S., Lloyd, K., Hawton, K. (2018). Self-harm, Suicidal Behaviours, and Cyberbullying in Children and Young People: Systemic review. *Journal of Medical Internet Research.* 20(4), 129-144.

Tuohy, W. (2019). Women Are Still Being Targeted Online 'at Their Weakest Point'. *The Sydney Morning Herald.* May 16.

How to avoid the traps of social media

Sternberg, R.J. (2001). Why Schools Should Teach for Wisdom: The balance theory of wisdom in educational settings. *Educational Psychologist*, 36(4), 227-245.

Reznitskaya, A., and Sternberg, R.J. (2004). Teaching Students to Make Wise Judgments: The 'Teaching for Wisdom' program. In: P.A. Linley, and S. Joseph (Eds.). *Positive Psychology in Practice.* Hoboken, NJ: John Wiley & Sons.

Conclusion

Wachowski, L., and Wachowski, L. (Dir.) (1999). *The Matrix.* Warner Bros.

Chapter 2: System 3 thinking explained

'How could people be so foolish?'

Scharmer, O. and Kaeufer, K. (2013). *Leading from the Emerging Future: From ego-system to eco-system economies.* San Francisco, CA: Berrett-Koehler Publishers.

The myth of rationality

Fowler, H.N. (1914). *Plato: Euthyphro, Apology, Crito, Phaedo, Phaedrus.* Greek with translation, Loeb Classical Library 36, Cambridge, MA: Harvard University Press.

Freud, S. (1923). *The Ego and the Id.* Vienna, Austria: Internationaler Psychoanalytischer Verlag.

Epstein, S. (1973). The Self-Concept Revisited, or a Theory of a Theory. *American Psychologist,* 28, 404-414.

Epstein, S. (1991). Cognitive-Experiential Self-Theory: An integrative theory of personality. In R. C. Curtis (Ed.), *The relational self: Theoretical convergences in psychoanalysis and social psychology.* New York, NY: The Guilford Press.

Epstein, S. (1994). Integration of the Cognitive and the Psychodynamic Unconscious. *American Psychologist.* 49 (8), 709-724.

Denes-Raj, V., and Epstein, S. (1994). Conflict Between Intuitive and Rational Processing: When people behave against their better judgment. *Journal of Personality and Social Psychology,* 66(5), 819-829.

Epstein, S., Pacini, R., Denes-Raj, V., and Heier, H. (1996). Individual Differences in Intuitive-Experiential and Analytical-Rational Thinking Styles. *Journal of Personality and Social Psychology,* 71(2), 390-405.

Epstein, S. (2010). Demystifying Intuition: What it is, what it does, and how it does it. *Psychological Inquiry*, 21, 295-312.

Kahneman, D. (2011). *Thinking, Fast and Slow*. New York, NY: Farrar, Straus and Giroux.

Orton, J. (1969). *What the Butler Saw*. London, UK: Methuen.

Wilder, B., Diamond, A.I.L., and Breffort, A. (1963). *Irma la douce. A screenplay*. Gainesville, FL: Tower Publications, Inc.

Up or down?

Dijksterhuis, A. (2004). Think Different: The merits of unconscious thought in preference development and decision making. *Journal of Personality and Social Psychology*, 87, 586-598.

Hauser, M.C. (2006). *Moral Minds: How nature designed our universal sense of right and wrong*. New York, NY: HarperCollins Publishers.

Finding wisdom

Kunzmann, U., and Baltes, P. (2005). The Psychology of Wisdom: Theoretical and empirical challenges. In: R.J. Sternberg, and J. Jordan (Eds.) *A Handbook of Wisdom: Psychological Perspectives*. New York, NY: Cambridge University Press.

Oakes, H., Brienza, J.P., Elnakouri, A., and Grossmann, I. (2019). Wise Reasoning: Converging evidence for the psychology of sound judgement. In: R.J. Sternberg, and J. Glück (Eds.) *The Cambridge Handbook of Wisdom*. Cambridge, UK: Cambridge University Press.

Grossmann, I. (2017). Wisdom and How to Cultivate It: Review of emerging evidence for a constructivist model of wise thinking. *European Psychologist*, 22(4), 233-246.

Wen, S.W., Ryan, P., Ryan, C.A. (2016). Systems 1 and 2 Thinking Processes and Cognitive Reflection Testing in Medical Students. *Canadian Medical Education Journal*, 7(2), e97-e103.

Thorsteinson, T.J., and Withrow, S. (2009). Does Unconscious Thought Outperform Conscious Thought on Complex Decisions? A further examination. *Judgment and Decision Making*, 4(3), 235-247.

Baltes, P.B., and Freund, A.M. (2003). The Intermarriage of Wisdom and Selective Optimisation with Compensation: Two metaheuristics guiding the conduct of life. In: C. Keyes, and J. Haidt (Eds.). *Flourishing: Positive Psychology and the Life Well-Lived*. Washington, DC: American Psychological Association.

Baltes, P.B., and Smith, J. (1990). Toward a Psychology of Wisdom and its Ontogenesis. In: R.J. Sternberg (Ed.) *Wisdom: Its Nature, Origins, and Development*. Cambridge, UK: Cambridge University Press.

Staudinger, U.M., and Leipold, B. (2003). The Assessment of Wisdom-related Performance. In: S.J. Lopez, and C.R. Snyder (Eds.). *Positive Psychological Assessment: A Handbook of Models and Measures*. Washington, DC: American Psychological Association.

The third system of thinking

Meeks, T.W., and Jeste, D.V. (2009). Neurobiology of Wisdom: A Literature Overview, *Archives of General Psychiatry*, 66(4), 355-365.

Thomas, M.L., Martin, A.S., Eyler, L., Lee, E.E., Macagno, E., Devereaux, M., Chiong, W., and Jeste, D.V. (2019). Individual Differences in Level of Wisdom are Associated with Brain Activation During a Moral Decision-making Task. *Brain and Behavior*, 9(6), e01302.

Lee, E.E., and Jeste, D.V. (2019). Neurobiology of Wisdom. In: R.J. Sternberg, and J. Glück (Eds.) *The Cambridge Handbook of Wisdom*. Cambridge, UK: Cambridge University Press.

Gronchi, G., and Giovanelli, F. (2018). Dual Process Theory of Thought and Default Mode Network: A possible neural foundation of fast thinking. *Frontiers in Psychology*, 9(1237), 1-4.

Sormaz, M., Murphy, C., Wang, H-T., Hymers, M., Karapanagiotidis, T., Poerio, G., Margulies, D.S., Jefferies, E., Smallwood, J. (2018). Default Mode Network can Support the Level of Detail in Experience During Active Task States. *Proceedings of the National Academy of Sciences*, 115(37), 9318-9323.

The six dimensions of system 3 thinking

Thomas, M.L., Bangen, K.J., Palmer, B.W., Martin, A.S., Avanzino, J.A., Depp, C.A., Glorioso, D., Daly, R., and Jeste, D.V. (2017). A New Scale for Assessing Wisdom Based on Common Domains and a Neurobiological Model: The San Diego Wisdom Scale (SD-WISE). *Journal of Psychiatric Research*, 108, 40-47.

Glück, J., König, S., Naschenweng, K., Redzanowski, U., Dorner, L., Straßer, I., and Wiedermann, W. (2013). How to Measure Wisdom: Content, reliability, and validity of five measures. *Frontiers in Psychology*, 4, article 405.

Brienza, J.P., Kung, F.Y.H., Santos, H.C., Bobocel, D.R., and Grossmann, I. (2017). Wisdom, Bias, and Balance: Toward a process-sensitive measurement of wisdom-related cognition. *Journal of Personality and Social Psychology*. 115(6), 1093-1126.

Webb, P.J. (2017). Making Wise Decisions: How to improve your odds of making the right decisions for the right people at the right time! *Banking Insight*, January/February, 56-59.

Webb, P.J. (2018). Coaching for Wisdom. In: K. Brush, and I. Sobolewska (Eds.) *8th EMCC International Mentoring, Coaching, and Supervision Research Conference*, European Coaching and Mentoring Council, Brussels, Belgium.

Webb, P.J. (2020). Coaching for Wisdom: System 3 Thinking in Complex Decision Making. *Philosophy of Coaching: An International Journal.* 5(1), 113-128.

Chapter 3: How to enhance your system 3 thinking

Pad man

Gupta, R. (2014). The 100 Most Influential People: Arunachalam Muruganantham. *Time Magazine*, April 23.

Balki, R. (Dir.) (2018). *Pad Man.* Sony Pictures.

The two key practices that will help you enhance focus

Set up a regular practice of mindfulness

Hougaard, R., and Carter, J. (2018). *The Mind of the Leader: How to Lead Yourself, Your People, and Your Organization for Extraordinary Results.* Boston, MA: Harvard Business School Publishing.

Webb, P.J. (2015). Effects of Mindfulness Training on Workplace Performance. In: *Australian Psychological Society Limited, 11th Industrial and Organisational Psychology Conference*, Melbourne VIC, July 2-4.

Karunamuni, N. & Weerasekera, R. (2019). Theoretical Foundations to Guide Mindfulness Meditation: A path to wisdom. *Current Psychology*, 38, 627-646.

Hit the 'pause button' before making a big decision

Grossmann, I., Oakes, H., and Santos, H.C. (2019). Wise Reasoning Benefits from Emodiversity, Irrespective of Emotional Intensity. *Journal of Experimental Psychology: General*, 148(5), 805-823.

How to enhance life experience

Baltes, P.B., Staudinger, U.M., and Lindenberger, U. (1999). Lifespan Psychology: Theory and application to intellectual functioning. *Annual Review of Psychology.* 50, 471-507

Ardelt, M. (2005). How Wise People Cope with Crises and Obstacles in Life. *ReVision*, 28(1), 7-19.

Ardelt, M., and Jeste, D.V. (2018). Wisdom and Hard Times: The ameliorating effect of wisdom on the negative association between adverse life events and well-being. *The Journals of Gerontology Series B: Psychological Sciences and Social Sciences.* 73(8), 1374-1383.

Crossing a few dry gullies

Lion, P., and Marszalek, J. (2013). Anger and Disgust at Army Sex Scandal as 'Jedi Council' Emerges. *News.com.au:* June 14.

The two key practices that will help you enhance life experience

Reflect on the lessons of success and failure from your own life

Kilburg, R.R. (2006). *Executive Wisdom: Coaching and the emergence of virtuous leaders.* Washington, DC: American Psychological Association.

Reflect on the biographies of others and what it means to live a meaningful life

Kennedy, E.M. (2009). *True Compass: A memoir.* New York, NY: Hachette Book Group.

Benedict, J., and Keteyian, A. (2018). *Tiger Woods.* New York, NY: Simon & Schuster.

Walsh, D. (2012). *The Program: Seven deadly sins – my pursuit of Lance Armstrong.* London, UK: Simon & Schuster.

Yousafzai, M., and Lamb, C. (2014). *I Am Malala: The girl who stood up for education and was shot by the Taliban.* London, UK: Weidenfeld & Nicholson.

Vance, A. (2015). *Elon Musk: How the billionaire CEO of SpaceX and Tesla is shaping our future.* London, UK: Ebury Publishing.

Schultz, H., and Yang, D.J. (1997). *Pour Your Heart Into It: How Starbucks built a company one cup at a time.* New York, NY: Hyperion Books.

Clark, D. (2016). *Alibaba: The house that Jack Ma built.* London, UK: HarperCollins Publishers.

Tuchman, B.W. (1984). *The March of Folly: From Troy to Vietnam.* New York, NY: Ballantine Books.

Marsden, J. (Ed.) (1996). *This I Believe: Over 100 eminent Australians explore life's big question.* Sydney, NSW: Random House.

Zuckerman, A., and Vlack, A. (Ed.) (2008). *Wisdom.* Auckland, NZ: PQ Blackwell Limited.

How to enhance decisiveness

Cassidy, C. (2017). *Wisdom Profiles: Dilip Jeste.* London, UK: Evidence-based Wisdom Project.

Molecules of emotion

Pert, C.B. (1997). *Molecules of Emotion: Why you feel the way you feel.* New York, NY: Scribner.

The two key practices that will help you enhance decisiveness

Make smaller decisions building up to a big one: fail fast, frequently, and frugally

Hill, L.A., Brandeau, G., Truelove, E., and Lineback, K. (2014). *Collective Intelligence: The art and practice of leading innovation.* Boston, MA: Harvard Business Review Press.

Galliott, K. (2020). View from the Top: Pip Marlow. *QANTAS Magazine.* January.

How to enhance compassion

Gyatso, T., and Hopkins, J. (Transl.) (2000). *The Meaning of Life: Buddhist perspectives on cause & effect.* Somerville, MA: Wisdom Publications.

Jinpa, T. (Transl. and Ed.) (2005). *Essence of the Heart Sutra: The Dalai Lama's heart of wisdom teachings.* Somerville, MA: Wisdom Publications.

Jinpa, T. (Transl. and Ed.) (2005). *Practicing Wisdom: The perfection of Shantideva's Bodhisattva Way.* Sommerville, MA: Wisdom Publications.

Under the Bodhi tree

Wallace, A.B. (2006). *The Attention Revolution: Unlocking the power of the focused mind.* Somerville, MA: Wisdom Publications.

Wallace, A.B. (2012). *Meditations of a Buddhist Skeptic: A manifesto for the mind sciences and contemplative practice.* New York, NY: Columbia University Press.

How to enhance emotional regulation

David, S. (2016). *Emotional Agility.* London, UK: Penguin Random House.

The two key practices that will help you enhance emotional regulation
Identify and name what you're feeling as emotions arise

Rohr, R. (2011). *Falling Upward: A spirituality for the two halves of life.* San Francisco, CA: Jossey-Bass.

Don't take things personally: acknowledge others' emotional responses without taking responsibility for them

Ruiz, M.A. (1997). *The Four Agreements: A practical guide to personal freedom.* San Rafael, CA: Amber-Allen Publishing.

The two key practices that will help you enhance tolerance for divergent values

Notice what triggers a judgmental response in you and seek to be more flexible

Böhmig-Krumhaar, S.A., Staudinger U.M., and Baltes, P.B. (2002). In Search of More Tolerance: Testing the facilitative effect of a knowledge-activating mnemonic strategy on value relativism. *Journal of Developmental Psychology and Educational Psychology.* 34, 30-43.

Glück, J., and Baltes, P.B. (2006). Using the Concept of Wisdom to Enhance the Expression of Wisdom Knowledge: Not the philosopher's dream but differential effects of developmental preparedeness. *Psychology and Aging*, 21(4), 679-690.

Chapter 4: When choices go bad

Thomas, G. (2019). From the Archives: The Ansett collapse. *Australian Aviation.* September 14.

When the world economy almost collapsed

Knauff, M., Budeck, C., Wolf, A.G., Hamburger, K. (2010). The Illogicality of Stock-Brokers: Psychological experiments on the effects of prior knowledge and belief biases on logical reasoning in stock trading. *Plos One.* 5(10), e13483.

The Sydney light rail gets heavy

Davies, A. (2018). Sydney's Light Rail Chaos: Who is to blame for delays and costly blowout? *The Guardian Australia.* April 21.

Nutt, P.C. (2002). *Why Decisions Fail: Avoiding the blunders and traps that lead to debacles.* San Francisco, CA: Berrett-Koehler Publishers.

Bad bankers

Ferguson, A. (2019). *Banking Bad.* Sydney, NSW: HarperCollins Publishers.

The Boeing nosedive

Useem, J. (2019). The Long-forgotten Flight that Sent Boeing Off Course. *The Atlantic.* November 20.

Langewiesche, W. (2019). What Really Brought Down the Boeing 737 Max? *The New York Times Magazine.* September 18.

Gelles, D. (2020). 'I Honestly Don't Trust Many People at Boeing': A broken culture exposed. *The New York Times.* January 10.

Duncan, I., Laris, M., and Aratani, L. (2020). Boeing 7373 Max Crashes Were 'Horrific Culmination' of Errors, Investigators Say. *The Washington Post.* September 17.

Kay, J. (2011). *Obliquity: Why our goals are best achieved indirectly.* London, UK: Profile Books.

Conclusion

Lumet, S. (Dir.) (1976). *Network.* United Artists

Chapter 5: The WISE framework for making better decisions

Why you need a decision making framework

Pascoe, B. (2014). *Dark Emu: Aboriginal Australia and the birth of agriculture.* Broome, WA: Magabala Books.

How to WIDEN your view of the problem

O'Connell, B. (2012). *Solution-Focused Therapy (Brief Therapy Series)*, 3rd Edition. London, UK: Sage Publications.

How to INTERROGATE THE REALITY of the situation
Get WISE

The four critical questions that will interrogate reality

Martin, R. (2009). *The Opposable Mind: How successful leaders win through integrative thinking.* Boston, MA: Harvard Business School Publishing.

How to ENACT A WAY FORWARD without procrastinating

Set a clear intention as the first step

Coelho, P. (1987). *The Pilgrimage: A contemporary quest for ancient wisdom.* London, UK: HarperCollins.

Chapter 6: Creating a brighter future

The greatest city in the world

West, S. (Dir.) (2001). *Lara Croft; Tomb Raider.* Paramount Pictures.

Is it harder to be wise now?

Orwell, G. (1949). *1984.* London, UK: Secker & Warburg.

Tuchman, B.W. (1984). *The March of Folly: From Troy to Vietnam.* New York, NY: Ballantine Books.

Tainter, J. (1990). *The Collapse of Complex Societies. New studies in archaeology.* Cambridge, UK: Cambridge University Press.

Turchin, P. (2018). *Historical Dynamics: Why states rise and fall.* Princeton, NJ: Princeton University Press.

Turchin, P., and Hoyer, D. (2020). *Figuring Out the Past: The 3,495 vital statistics that explain world history.* London, UK: Profile Books.

Strauss, W., and Howe, N. (1997). *The Fourth Turning: An American prophecy.* New York, NY: Broadway Books.

Planting seeds of wisdom in a field of ignorance

Wheatley, M.J. (2017). *Who Do We Choose To Be? Facing reality, claiming leadership, restoring sanity.* San Francisco, CA: Berrett-Koehler Publishers.

Developing a practice of wisdom

Sternberg, R.J. (1998). A Balance Theory of Wisdom. *Review of General Psychology*, 2, 347-365.

Baltes, P., and Staudinger, U. (2000). Wisdom: A metaheuristic to orchestrate mind and virtue toward excellence. *American Psychologist*, 55(1), 122-136.

Keyes, C.L.M. & Haidt, J. (2003). Human Flourishing: The study of that which makes life worthwhile. In: C.L.M. Keyes & J. Haidt (Eds.). *Flourishing: Positive Psychology and the Life Well-Lived.* Washington DC: American Psychological Association.

Ardelt, M. (2004). Wisdom as Expert Knowledge System: A critical review of a contemporary operationalization of an ancient concept. *Human Development.* 47(5), 257-285.

Sternberg, R.J. (2004). What is Wisdom and How Can We Develop It? *The Annals of the American Academy of Political and Social Science*, 591,164-174.

Birren, J.E. & Fisher, L.M. (2005). The Elements of Wisdom: Overview and integration. In: R.J. Sternberg & J. Jordan (Eds.) *A Handbook of Wisdom: Psychological Perspectives.* New York, NY: Cambridge University Press.

Sternberg, R.J. (2005). Foolishness. In: R.J. Sternberg & J. Jordan (Eds.) *A Handbook of Wisdom: Psychological perspectives.* New York, NY: Cambridge University Press.

Kilburg, R.R. (2006). *Executive Wisdom: Coaching and the emergence of virtuous leaders.* Washington, DC: American Psychological Association.

Nonaka, I. & Takeuchi, H. (2011). The Wise Leader: How CEOs can learn practical wisdom to help them do what's right for their companies – and society. *The Harvard Business Review*, May.

Grossmann, I., Na, J., Varnum, M.E.W., Kitayama, S., Nisbett, R.E. (2013). A Route to Well-being: Intelligence vs. Wise Reasoning. *Journal of Experimental Psychology: General*, 142(3), 944–953.

Intezari, A. & Puleen, D.J. (2013). Students of Wisdom: An integral meta-competencies theory of practical wisdom. In: W.M. Küpers & D.J. Puleen (Eds.). *A Handbook of Practical Wisdom: Leadership, Organization and Integral Business Practice*. Aldershot, UK: Gower Publishing.

Grossmann, I. (2017). Wisdom in context. *Perspectives on Psychological Science*. 12(2), 233-257.

McKenna, B. & Rooney, D. (2019). Wise leadership. In: R.J. Sternberg & J. Glück (Eds.) *The Cambridge Handbook of Wisdom*. Cambridge, UK: Cambridge University Press.

Sternberg, R.J. (2019). Race to Samara: The Critical Importance of Wisdom in the World Today. In: R.J. Sternberg & J. Glück (Eds.) *The Cambridge Handbook of Wisdom*. Cambridge, UK: Cambridge University Press.

Gilbert, P. (2013). *The Compassionate Mind: A New Approach to Life's Problems*. London, UK: Constable & Robinson Ltd.

Rohr, R. (2011). *Falling Upward: A spirituality for the two halves of life*. San Francisco, CA: Jossey-Bass.

Conclusion: Your moment of choice

Roy, A. (1999). *The Cost of Living: The greater common good and the end of imagination*. Hammersmith, UK: Flamingo.